If They Only Knew

A COP'S JOURNEY WITH ADDICTION AND MENTAL HEALTH

A Memoir

LANCE VALCOUR

MILNER &
ASSOCIATES INC
· EDITING · PUBLISHING · COMMUNICATIONS · CONSULTING ·

Excerpt from *Meet Joe Black* courtesy of Universal Studios Licensing LLC.

ISBN 978-1-988344-49-2 (paperback)
ISBN 978-1-988344-50-8 (e-book)

Production Credits
Editor and project manager: Karen Milner
Copy editor: Lindsay Humphreys
Interior design and typesetting: Adrian So, AdrianSoDesign
Cover design: Adrian So, AdrianSoDesign
Front cover photo (sunrise): Lance Valcour

Published by Milner & Associates Inc.
www.milnerassociates.ca

Praise for *If They Only Knew*

"Many of those currently serving in the law enforcement profession will, at some point in their careers, struggle with depression, addiction or other forms of at-risk behavior. . . . Lance summoned the inner strength to recognize his issues and worked hard to address them head on before they destroyed him, his family and his career. It is my sincere hope that law enforcement officers (and their families) everywhere take the time to read Lance's story."

    —Christopher M. Moore, Chief of Police (Ret.),
    San Jose Police Department

"This book was a powerful reminder that you can never truly know the battles someone faces behind closed doors or in the quiet of their mind. . . . For anyone struggling—whether with addiction, mental health or the weight of their responsibilities—this book is an essential read. It offers hope, demonstrating that with the right changes and a solid support system, life can and will get better."

    —Matthew Cox, President-CEO, Ottawa Police Association

"Lance's experience demonstrates the impact that our co-founder, Sister Louise, had on so many individuals' lives. Today we have modernized Serenity Renewal for Families but have stayed loyal to the core principles. We continue her legacy by supporting individuals and families affected directly or indirectly by addictions."

    —Neil M. Leslie, Executive Director, Serenity Renewal for Families

"People have often asked me, as a long-lived trauma survivor, how it is that we as police officers can successfully use our experience as front-line saviours to the public, yet at the same time use that same experience to destroy our family relationships. Lance gives us a wonderful view of how this can happen. We work in an environment where everything is controlled by policies, procedures and guidelines; but at home, in family life, there are no such guardrails, and when opinions clash it is seen as a challenge. The most wonderful thing about Lance's reveal is its honesty—a willingness to see oneself in a mirror."

    —Syd Gravel, Retired Staff Sergeant, Ottawa Police;
    officer wellness advocate; author of *56 Seconds*

"If They Only Knew *is a compelling read that resonates with anyone seeking to understand the intricacies of addiction, mental health and the often unseen burdens carried by first responders.*"

—Harry Tangye, *Retired Police Sergeant (England) and author of* Firearms and Fatals

"*An incredible story of one man's private struggles with addiction and mental health, and the courage it took not only to survive, but to share this journey with others.*"

—*Chief (Ret.) Andrew Fletcher, M.O.M. South Simcoe Police Service FBINAA*

"*A deeply personal and unflinching reflection on thirty years of policing. Valcour lays bare the slow creep of his own mental illness and addiction in a profession where personal struggles are often buried beneath a veneer of control and competence.* If They Only Knew *is a testament to the beauty of love, courage and humility.*"

—*Patrick F. Parnaby PhD, Associate Professor of Sociology, University of Guelph*

"*Lance's candid, raw, and generous exploration of mental illness, addiction, suicide and the pressures of high-impact policing reveals a deeply human story that resonates universally. . . . his journey reminds us that even the boy next door could be quietly battling unimaginable struggles. Alongside his wife, Lise, Lance earns admiration and respect as they break their silence, share their story, and reclaim their lives from the grip of shame and stigma surrounding mental health.*"

—*Lisa MacLeod, mental health advocate, former cabinet minister and cookbook author*

To Garry A., for showing me the way, Dr. Joe Dietrich for telling me the truth, and Sister Louise for not putting up with my BS.

To Jonny, Dominic and Mat for all the pain I've caused.

Most of all, to Lise, for her incredible strength, courage and perseverance, without which this journey would have ended long ago.

Contents

Foreword

At a time when we are increasingly confronted with the devastating news of police suicides and mounting research on the mental health challenges faced by law enforcement officers, Lance Valcour's wonderful new book, *If They Only Knew: A Cop's Journey with Addiction and Mental Health*, is especially timely and necessary. His candid account of battling addiction and mental health issues peels back the polished veneer of a decorated police career with the Ottawa Police Service, revealing a vulnerable and deeply human side of a profession often shrouded in silence about such struggles.

If They Only Knew is a raw, heart-wrenching and ultimately uplifting journey into the depths of one man's struggle with addiction and mental health, and the power of redemption. As someone who has read many books written by those who have struggled with these issues, none have gripped me with the same intensity as Lance's story. What struck me most was the honesty in his reflections—not just about his personal failings, but also about the toll it took on his family.

This is more than a memoir of struggle, however; it is a testament to resilience, love and the healing power of truth. The strength and courage of his wife, who refused to let their marriage and their family spiral downward any further, are as integral to this story as Lance's eventual road to recovery. Their determination to rebuild their lives offers a powerful and inspirational message of hope for any couple facing similar challenges. While reading about their journey, I cried, I laughed, I got angry and I reflected deeply on the complexities of addiction, mental health and the human spirit. Lance's story proves that it's never too late to confront your demons, seek help and find peace.

This book also sheds light on the systemic issue of addiction and mental health within policing. Police officers, tasked with confronting humanity's worst moments daily, shoulder an enormous emotional burden that sadly goes unseen and unaddressed far too often. Lance's story is a reminder that these hidden struggles can have devastating consequences for officers and their families—but also that recovery, support and understanding can save lives.

If They Only Knew is a must-read for anyone searching for a story of redemption or a reminder that even in our darkest moments, there is always a path towards light. It will help police officers and other first responders who are struggling with their own addiction and/ or mental health challenges. It will also be an invaluable resource for researchers who study first-responder wellness and for clinicians who work with these individuals on their road to recovery.

I will be making *If They Only Knew* required reading for all of my students. For these students, Lance's story will serve as a critical reminder that behind every data point in studies about addiction and mental health, there are real people with complex lives, families and deep struggles. We must never forget that these statistics represent individuals whose pain and stories deserve to be heard and understood.

Craig Bennell, PhD
Professor, Department of Psychology, Carleton University
Director, Police Research Lab

Preface

If they only knew who I really was and what I had done; how I had taken such a beautiful spirit and caged it for years through anger, abuse and manipulation, they could never truly accept me.

Lance Valcour April 2020

Those words are the hardest I have ever communicated. Hardest because they are absolutely true and an accurate reflection of how I treated my wife, Lise, who is such a beautiful person, both inside and out. She was never deserving of the pain and suffering I put her through for so many years. No one is, but especially not her.

On the surface, I was an accomplished professional; a police officer who had risen through the ranks to become an inspector. I was respected as an expert in technology and information management systems, speaking and providing advice to other police services all over Canada and around the world. But if they only knew. If my colleagues and clients—or even my extended family and friends—only knew what I was like in my private life, they wouldn't have respected me at all. If they only knew how I treated my family, especially my amazing wife, they would have loathed the monster I had become.

I suspect that many who read my opening words will immediately stop and put this book aside—thinking, possibly correctly, that reading a book written by someone like me is in some way supporting my past reprehensible behaviours.

My only response to that is similar to the one I once gave to a constable who called me out as being self-centred and selfish when I was promoted and took over his platoon: "You're right—but that was the *old* Lance Valcour. Please give me six months to show you who the new one is. If after six months you still feel that way, then I will understand. If, however, I show you that I have changed, then I would appreciate your new feedback." In the same spirit, I ask you not to judge me until you've read my whole story. Please know that I'm sharing it not to seek pity or forgiveness for my past behaviours, but to seek understanding for them. This is my story of change and redemption, and I hope that by sharing it, I can inspire others to face their struggles.

This book has been a long time in the making. Five years, in fact. It has been difficult to face who I became and how I treated those closest to me. To face a lifelong struggle with addiction and mental health issues. To admit to people who I truly was and to reveal in a very public way feelings and behaviours I am still not proud of. To re-seek forgiveness from Lise and our children, despite them having forgiven me long ago. Many stops and starts and family discussions later, what started as an intensely personal and family project is now ready to be shared more widely.

When I set out to write this book, I thought and hoped the process might be therapeutic for me, that it might help with the ongoing process of my recovery. My family's forgiveness, as mentioned, was also top of mind. In addition, I believed that sharing the details of our life—the good, bad and ugly—with our adult children (Lise knows them all too well) would be good for them—a cautionary tale, if nothing else. They knew most of the story, but not all.

Although at first I wasn't sure if I would ever publish this book, after multiple lengthy conversations with Lise, we decided to make our story public. We hoped that by sharing my story it might help other first responders, members of the military, their family members and anyone else who has struggled with despair, pain, addiction and mental health challenges. This hope was confirmed after I spoke publicly about my journey for the first time at a conference in the fall of 2023. The feedback from attendees was overwhelmingly positive with a consistent push to "Please publish your book—it will help many!"

I hoped, too, that somewhere in these pages I would also find self-forgiveness, which is something I still struggle with today.

For those of you who continue to read, please do so with an open mind and attempt to look beyond the ugliness to see the kind, giving young boy I once was; a boy desperate for love and acceptance. Seek understanding—the same understanding I am still attempting to find even after writing this book—about how that young boy grew into the sick, addicted, depressed and suicidal man that he became. What happened? Why did he become that man? What caused that terrible change? Then strive to understand the transformation that took place in that man, primarily due to the strength, love and courage of a woman. Witness their journey through the valley of despair to experiencing the joy and beauty of mountaintops around the world, literally and figuratively.

Ultimately, this is a love story However, it is also a story about pain, suffering, commitment, strength, courage and the will to persevere. It's about a journey to become interdependent and respectful. And to seek peace, serenity and acceptance, every day.

Chapter 1
The End?

I'm such a fucking asshole. They'll be better off without me. Lise will be able to find a kind and loving husband who will be a much better father for the boys. Yeah, they'll probably miss me for a while, but in time, they will move on and see this for what it is—the best for all of them.

This was my self-talk on and off for years, and the same kind of self-destructive thinking that drove me one horrible day to sit on the stairs to our basement, staring at my service gun. Here was where my recovery journey started, from a challenging and painful place full of misguided ideas and beliefs, resentment and anger, and overall anguish with all that felt wrong with me and around me.

As a veteran cop, I'd responded to numerous suicides. In every case, my number-one thought was: *What a weak and selfish person. Who could do this to their family?* Especially in cases where a person had killed themselves in their own home—forcing one of their family members to find them and then have to live with those memories forever. Not once did I ever think that they might be killing themselves in a misguided attempt to *help* their family.

Our relationship had become nothing but out-of-control fights, with me constantly yelling, swearing and emotionally abusing Lise.

I had never abused her physically, so in my mind, my behaviour was OK. In fact, if I'm truly honest, I thought she deserved my outbursts. *Why is she being such a bitch to me all the time? Doesn't she understand that I'm working my ass off for her and the kids? Why doesn't she get the fuck off my back?*

Thinking of killing myself was not a new concept. The idea of doing it had started creeping into the darkest corners of my mind months earlier, likely after another fight; another screaming match; another bout of feeling down, lonely and full of self-pity.

Everyone who knows and works with me sees me as being hugely successful, an up-and-coming star in the police force. Why doesn't she see it? I'm doing all of this for her, for our family. Fuck her if she thinks she can do better. She's probably planning on leaving me soon, anyway. She's just waiting for the right time financially so that she can take all my money and take off with the boys.

I was full of anger, resentment and distrust. On my darkest days, I would spend an entire shift driving around in my police car, thinking about how best to kill myself. I could say on the radio that I was in pursuit and then ram my police car into an abutment at 100 miles an hour. *That would do it.*

However, that night while sitting on the steps to our basement with my gun in my right hand, I felt no anger. No resentment. No distrust. Only love for Lise and the boys. *This is for the best. They'll be better off.*

Then Lise found me there. She was shocked and terrified, but she came and sat beside me. She held me and spoke softly, saying, "It's OK. Everything will be OK. We will get through this together. We need you, sweetheart. We love you and need you."

What was very nearly the end for me became a new beginning.

Chapter 2

Lemon Gin

Lemon gin changed my life forever.

In high school, a few of us got an older friend to buy us a mickey, about thirteen ounces, which we shared. It was like the elixir of the gods. It was like someone taking a key and unlocking my brain. I felt normal. I felt great. I fit in. I was accepted.

I loved it!

That first drunk, I guess I would have been about seventeen, was so much fun. My friend drove us to the next town over, Morrisburg, Ontario, and we went to the indoor rink. It was a Saturday night, I believe. There was public skating, but we didn't have our skates with us. No problem, we thought. We'll just run around on the ice in our boots!

Everyone thought we were funny—everyone except the rink manager, that is. We were laughing and enjoying ourselves. I wasn't worried about anything, not even what my mother would think or how disappointed she would be in me. *For the first time in my life*, I remember thinking, *I'm free to do whatever I want.* I wanted more of that feeling.

This began a pattern of behaviour that continued for the next twenty years. Drinking to relax or because I thought I deserved it for working hard or because something bad, or good, had happened at school or work or in life. I felt better when I drank. I felt more accepted. I was part of the group, not apart from it.

The feelings of guilt began early on and would only continue to grow as time went on. When I would wake up the next morning with a hangover, I knew that I hadn't behaved the way I was supposed to. I would feel guilty that I had disappointed my parents, especially my mother; her love and acceptance were of paramount concern to me in those early years, yet they always felt a little out of reach. I would also feel guilty that my actions were not what God wanted. (As you will read in the next chapter, God's opinion of my actions was also extremely important to me.)

I would tell myself that, next time, I would not drink so much or not behave as I did the last time. They say the road to hell is paved with good intentions. Well, I had lots of good intentions—and none of the willpower to follow through when it came to drinking. Little did I know just how far down that hellish road I would travel.

To be clear here, I was not drinking every day. I went to school or work without fail—although I believe I still hold the record at my small-town high school for the number of late days in a single year (I don't know the number, but it was almost every day). No, I drank mostly on weekends. I was lucky enough to have friends who also liked to drink and who had parents who were less strict than mine about it. I suppose you could call me a binge drinker.

I don't want this to become a "drunkalogue," telling all the stories of how drunk I got. However, it's important to share some of them to explain how bad my drinking became, and how quickly, at an early age.

Like the time three of us got into a bottle of tequila. My mom was away, I'm not sure where. I said goodbye to my dad after supper as he left for a Knights of Columbus meeting, and then I left home shortly after him to meet my friends and drink. We started chugging the bottle of booze, each taking our turn. I don't think it was even a full twenty-six-ounce bottle, just part of one.

What I didn't know until later was that my friends were only pretending to drink and, therefore, I had drunk almost all of what was in the bottle. I was sick as a dog (still can't stand even the thought or smell of tequila) and they brought me home and put me to bed, long before my dad got home from his meeting. I had been gone for only an hour or so and was already drunk as a skunk.

The next morning, I woke up with a splitting headache and feeling guilty for having drunk so much, so fast. I was worried about what my dad would say and if he would tell my mom. It must have been a Saturday morning because my dad was in the living room when I walked out of the bedroom. I started to complain about how I felt, and he said, in his fatherly way, "If you can't do the time, don't do the crime." That was it. I never forgot that event nor how awful I felt afterwards. But it did nothing to stop me from drinking.

My high school days were in the early 1970s, a time when the attitude towards drinking and driving was very different than it is now. Although it was illegal, it was still considered totally acceptable to drive around and have a few drinks. Not to get drunk, but to socialize. We called it "touring."

We would leave high school on a Friday afternoon, often skipping our last class, get someone to acquire some booze for us, and then drive all over the county on back roads, thereby limiting the chance the cops would find us.

In the summer, we would each buy a four-pack of Lonesome Charlie wine because it was the cheapest thing available. The wine would fit nicely into our backpacks, and off we would go on our motorcycles, touring the countryside with our buddies. I had a Honda CT70 with a top speed, downhill with a wind, of about 70 kilometres per hour. We imagined ourselves as some kind of roving motorcycle gang, but honestly, we were all too afraid to do anything truly stupid—other than drinking and driving, that is.

For me, and many of my peers, this kind of drinking and driving was harmless. It was normal, at least to us. Having said that, I continued to have an ongoing internal dialogue about drinking too much. I would wake up the next day feeling guilty for having gotten drunk again. However, my drinking, at least in my mind, had no impact on how I behaved towards others. At least not yet.

The biggest problem, I would learn much later in life, was *why* I drank—not how much or how often.

Chapter 3
In the Beginning

Beginnings matter.

Nature or nurture? Our "family of origin," as well as our experiences, both positive and negative, combine over the years to mould us into who we become. Some Eastern philosophies believe this process is based on energy, passed on from previous lives lived. I have no idea if that's true, but I know that my upbringing plays a critical role in my journey.

I was born in the Grace Hospital in Ottawa on October 11, 1957, just one week after the Soviet Union successfully launched the world's first spaceship, *Sputnik*, which orbited Earth for about three weeks sending radio signals that were listened to by people around the globe. This was the height of the Cold War, when, as I would find out years later, everyone was scared and thought the world might end at any time.

My parents were John Henry Valcour and Rosemary Valcour, née Tobin. Both were from the Kemptville area just south of Ottawa, and we lived on Jack Street in that small, but growing, community.

My dad had three brothers and one sister and grew up on a farm with Protestant parents. He was born in 1921, just a few years before the Great Depression, and lived a very basic and hard-working life.

These experiences helped shape his later years, as did his time spent fighting in World War II. He drove tanks in Italy and Holland but rarely talked about his time overseas, except to tell us about how they gave chocolate bars to starving Dutch kids after they liberated the Netherlands.

My mom was born in 1923 and was an only child living on the family farm. One of her uncles was known for being the town drunk while the other, Uncle Allan, was well-respected and worked for the Ottawa Railway Company (now called OC Transpo). She worked in an office in Ottawa during the war but then returned to being a housewife (as they were called then) and was very proud to stay home to raise her four kids. She was a staunch Catholic and ensured her family was raised in the faith.

Our life was, to the best of my recollection, pretty normal. We lived in Kemptville and, once I was old enough, I went to Holy Cross Catholic School. I remember having fun in the big schoolyard and not wanting for anything. My dad converted to Catholicism, possibly before I was born. He joined the Knights of Columbus and regularly went to their meetings, eventually becoming a Fourth Degree Grand Knight—their highest level, I'm told.

Dad was always around heavy machinery and drove his own dump truck for work after the war. He worked on the St. Lawrence Seaway system and on building the nuclear reactor in Chalk River, Ontario. I remember him telling us that, even as a war vet, he would be asked to show his identification every time he entered Chalk River. It upset him that the Soviets who came to visit the reactor were whisked into the area with no trouble. He always said that when the Allies had finished with Germany they should have kept going into the Soviet Union, as he considered them our biggest threat. (It was only after the Soviets were revealed to be stealing secrets, including nuclear secrets, that their access privileges in Chalk River were revoked!)

When my two brothers, our sister and I were growing up, Dad worked as a mechanic for a car dealership in Kemptville. He later got a job as the master mechanic at Cardinal Construction in Cardinal, Ontario, right along the St. Lawrence River. He drove about forty kilometres each way from Kemptville to Cardinal every day for years.

In 1967, when I was almost ten, our parents decided to move to Iroquois, Ontario, much closer to Dad's work in Cardinal, which saved him quite a bit of travel time every day. The sign at the edge of Iroquois proclaimed it the "Best Town by a Dam Site," because the entire village had been relocated next to the newly built dam during the building of the Seaway system and hydro projects in the 1950s. Families who wanted to keep their homes had them moved at no cost. Others got new homes, and that was what my parents bought for us, a nice little three-bedroom bungalow with a finished basement on Church Street. We could see the St. Lawrence River from our back window, with the huge ships coming and going and the United States on the other side of the river.

My oldest brother, Gary, did not make the move with us. He went to a private Catholic school in Grenville, near Brockville, for a couple of years before heading off to university. My sister Anita and I played *Monopoly* every day that summer and spent lots of time at the beach, where we would ride our bikes too. My brother Stew met another boy during our first mass as altar servers at St. Cecilia's Church and, after that, he was gone with his new friends all the time.

Stew and I started at St. Cecilia Catholic School that September while Anita attended Seaway District High School. Overall, I did OK academically in grade school, but I struggled with several subjects. My cursive handwriting was so bad that my teacher suggested printing everything, which I continue to do today.

I may not have been the best student, but to make up for it I was always helpful in school and became the audio-visual kid, getting the equipment out of storage and setting up the films for our teacher (it was fun to watch them backwards). I took a great deal of pride in being seen as such a helpful boy.

I continued to serve on the altar at church but was not very good at it. I fainted one Easter when holding the incense (not sure what happened). Another Easter, I had the honour of holding the crucifix at the front of the procession and proudly leading everyone back to the sacristy after mass—only to find out that mass was not over, which caused the priest to become pretty upset at me, as he had to get us turned around and lead everyone back into the church. My final blunder was when I was putting several lit candles onto the altar in front of the entire congregation. The base of the stand hit the altar, and all the candles went flying, breaking everywhere.

In our second summer in Iroquois, I took up golf and loved the sport for the freedom it gave me. I could ride my bike, pulling my seven-club set of Pin High golf clubs on a cart behind me, from our house to the third tee, and I played every day.

When I wasn't golfing, I was either swimming at the beach, playing tennis, fishing, exploring on my bike or out shooting with my pellet gun. My dad had been a hunter and took us fishing on Georgian Bay once. I loved hunting and fishing, again for the liberty they gave me.

It was a wonderful time in my life, when I could pretty much do anything I wanted—as long as I followed my parent's rules, was home every evening to say the rosary and did the dishes after dinner. Breaking the rules had real consequences. I once suggested to some kids that they let the air out of another kid's bicycle in an attempt to get him back for some perceived slight. When my dad found out, he whipped me with an extension cord, raising welts on my butt that were there for days. He said the punishment was going to be harder for him than it was for me. I didn't think so at the time, but I now realize that he was doing his best to keep me from engaging in bad behaviour that could eventually lead to me breaking the law. I'm not condoning what he did, but it certainly drove me to stick to his rules and respect the law.

In grade school, I received corporal punishment a couple of times with the principal whacking my hand with a ruler. I started crying before she hit me, saying that I wasn't crying because of what she was about to do but because of what would happen to me when I got home. I don't remember those consequences now; I'm sure my mom punished me, but I don't recall anything major. Maybe she didn't want to tell my dad because of the whipping I had received in the past. I wish she was still around so I could ask her.

We were raised very strictly as Catholics. Everything was a sin. I lived in fear all the time of going to hell if I did something wrong. I remember going to mass every Sunday morning and listening to the sermon. It was, at least in my mind, all about sin and what would happen if we broke the rules. On the way home from church, Mom would give us another sermon and explain everything the priest had told us (fortunately, it was a short car ride home).

We would have breakfast together after church, and my dad always had one beer with his. It was like a tradition, and, as far as I can remember, it was the only time I saw him drink alcohol while I was growing up. I guess he was as good at hiding things as I later became. After doing the dishes and any homework we had, we kids were free to do as we pleased. It was great growing up in a village of about 1,100 people, as we had no fear about cycling everywhere and, in our minds at least, there was nothing that could hurt us in our beautiful little town.

Once I got to high school, things got both better and worse. Better in the sense that I was fairly athletic and got to play on school sports teams, primarily basketball and volleyball, and through that, I made a few friends. I was also a pretty good goalie for our town hockey team, and we did quite well for such a small village. However, I was very socially awkward and fixated on never breaking the rules— any rules. I was the only kid in Grade 9 with a brush cut, mostly because it made my mom happy. Everyone else, like my brother Stew, who was in Grade 11, had long hair, as was the style.

My two older siblings were gone by now, so they were less of a role model for me at this early stage of my life. Instead, I watched Stew in action, both on and off the court (he was the star of the teams he played on), and, unconsciously, wondered why everything was so easy for him: great athlete, great marks and everyone liked him. I was always very introverted, felt uncomfortable in almost every social setting (except on the court, where I became one of the better players) and rarely knew what to say or how to say it—especially with girls.

• • •

One part of my personality that I did not understand at the time, and which became important later in life, was my absolute terror of dying. I have no idea why I felt this way, but even the thought of it would cause me to almost feel physically sick and I would walk around the house talking to myself, demanding that my brain stop thinking about it.

I suppose this was a form of panic attack but, of course, I had no idea what was happening or what that term might have meant back then. I just knew that the thought of dying scared the living crap out of me, and I would do anything I could not to think about it. While I can manage this fear better today, I still feel anxious just writing the words here.

A similar, but unrelated, phobia of mine was the fear of losing my parents. Again, I don't know where this came from, but perhaps it was because I often felt that my mother was distant and emotional-ly unavailable to me. I would do anything to gain her attention and approval, and I would feel unbelievably guilty if I had displeased her even mildly. Don't get me wrong, it's not like she was ice-cold or any-thing. In fact, when putting our two-and-a-half-year-old grandson to bed recently, I was holding him as he started to fall asleep, rubbing and scratching his back. I told him that my mother used to do the same thing when I would ask her, "Itch me, scratch me, tickle me, Momma." Such a fond memory of how safe and secure I felt in the cocoon of our family. In any event, at times I fixated on the idea of losing my mother and father entirely.

I remember getting home from school one day (I don't remem-ber how old I was, but it was likely around Grade 7 or 8) and my mother called me into the living room saying she had something to tell me. She was sitting there with a serious look on her face. She started to tell me that she and Dad were getting divorced. She didn't get all the words out of her mouth before I was on the floor crying and losing it.

Mom quickly came to me and told me that she had just been kidding and that she and Dad weren't getting divorced. It took a few minutes for her to convince me, but eventually, I calmed down and told her never to do that to me again. I have no idea what prompted her to want to pull such a terrible trick on me, but I still remember that moment when I thought my world was ending.

The idea that the foundation of my life—my family—might be unstable and possibly crumbling around me left me feeling off-kilter, a feeling I would later face on a regular basis.

• • •

My scholastic abilities in Grade 9 were poor. I was already beginning to fall behind in key building-block classes like math and science. By the time I was in Grade 11, I rarely understood anything the teachers were saying. It was like they were talking Greek to me.

In addition, I would sometimes transpose numbers, which only compounded my issues with math-related subjects at school. My mind just could not comprehend the complex mathematical questions I was beginning to be exposed to, resulting in me falling further and further behind. Others in my classes seemed to have the special "key" required to unlock these puzzles, while I couldn't even seem to find where the key went, let alone find the right one to fit each lock.

As a result, I started to act out, becoming a bit of a class comedian. This got me sent to the office fairly regularly, but that made me happy because I didn't have to sit in the classroom pretending to know the answers to questions that everyone else seemed to be able to solve easily.

In math class, I would bring a comic book and put it inside my textbook to read while the teacher was lecturing from the front of the class. I could not control all the thoughts that were running around in my mind. It was as if there were a mouse constantly running on a wheel in my head. I couldn't shut it off.

I felt lost. I felt stupid. I felt worthless.

I knew my marks were a concern for my parents. I believe my mom did her best to help, but nothing seemed to make any sense to me. It was like my brain was wired differently than everyone else's and nothing I tried could decipher the messages my teachers were sending me.

• • •

Summertime was the best, as it is for most kids. I had to work, first at odd jobs around the house and then later in summer jobs, but the free time was fantastic. And the break from the rigours and frustrations of schoolwork was liberating.

The money I earned, both as a lifeguard and a carry-out boy at the local store, was great and allowed me to save up for what I wanted to buy. In the winter, I was a hockey referee, again earning some extra money—almost all of which I saved. My mom was always talking about how much I had accumulated, and I felt proud to hear her talking about me in such a positive fashion. Anything I could do to earn praise from my mother was fantastic!

Both the lifeguarding and refereeing began to develop my ability to control situations. I liked that feeling of power, as I was not a very powerful person in other parts of my life. I didn't consciously think about these things then, and only decades later did I realize that those two jobs fit into a much larger pattern; but even in my youth, the need to have control of things was something that I naturally gravitated to. I believed it was both important and necessary for the health and safety of the people I was there to guard at the beach or to manage, in the case of hockey. However, when improperly used and allowed to take over other parts of my life, my desire for control over situations, and people, could and would eventually lead to very negative results.

My lifeguarding and grocery store jobs proved important in my life in another way. They brought me into contact with the local police, the Ontario Provincial Police (OPP). They would pull up to the front of the store or park at the beach and get out to chat. I asked tons of questions and, after turning sixteen, was allowed to go on multiple ride-alongs (different rules back then).

I loved everything about what they did. They seemed to help people. They seemed respected. People listened to what they said. This was the career I wanted. I knew it with all my heart by the time I was seventeen years old. I just needed to wait until I was twenty-one, the minimum hiring age for the OPP.

But what would I do for a job until then? My marks were so poor that there was no way I was going to university. I explored the idea of driving transport trucks. My mom was very wise, so she pretended to go along with the idea. She got a neighbour who drove a big shiny transport truck to take me on the longest, most boring, run he had. That cured me of that idea pretty quickly.

One summer, I worked as a mason's helper. That was, by far, the most difficult job physically I've ever worked at. I was in fantastic shape at the end of the summer, but I learned that physical work was not something I wanted to do for a career. Besides, I already knew what I wanted to be. I just had to wait until I was twenty-one to do it.

At seventeen years old, I had both my motorcycle and vehicle driver's licence and had a great deal of freedom with my small 70cc Honda for the summer and my dad's car pretty much whenever I wanted it. Other than my parents always after me to do better in school, things were going pretty well.

I was even going on the odd date but was far too nervous to try the things my friends were telling me about. Plus, if that went too far, I knew it would lead to sin and pregnancy. This was made abundantly clear at church on Sunday and in the many supplemental sermons from my mom.

You will note that I don't talk about my dad much during this phase of my life. That's because he was gone most of the time, working for a construction company that built roads all over Ontario. When he was home, he would always work late and then come home, eat the dinner my mother had prepared and then go watch TV. While he was a tremendous role model when it came to his strength, wisdom and service, especially during the war, his influence was diminished at this stage of my life due to his many absences.

What I didn't know then was *why* he was gone so many evenings.

Chapter 4
Spreading Wings

I may hold another record from Seaway District High School: the lowest average when graduating Grade 13 (which existed in Ontario back then)—52 percent. The only reason it was that high was because I took music and played the C flute. I loved it (and want to get back into playing) and got 90 percent in that class.

Years later, I was invited to speak at Johns Hopkins School of Applied Physics. I was there to lecture to a room filled with university researchers, most of them likely having earned their PhD or some other advanced degree in physics, or who had multiple advanced degrees.

The key message in my presentation was the importance of engaging the first-responder community *before* deciding on any public safety–related research topics. At this stage of my career, I had worked with dozens of researchers on a wide range of public safety research gaps. They would often reveal to us some fantastic new idea or solution—a true eureka moment for them and their career. The problem was that even when they explained their idea in layperson's language, we were often left scratching our heads wondering what problem they were trying to solve. In many cases, there were no practical applications for their "applied" research.

In any event, there I was, standing in a room filled with very smart, very educated people as well as a large group of my peers from policing and public safety. I decided to be honest with them and said, "Before I begin, I need to be very open with you about my educational background. I never went to university. My marks were nowhere near good enough. In fact, when I was in high school, I got 70 percent in physics and chemistry."

There was an almost audible gasp in the room when these highly educated experts realized they were about to be lectured to by someone who not only had no doctorate, nor even a masters, but who had received such a lowly grade in the subjects they held so dearly.

I continued: "It gets worse. The truth is that I actually got 35 percent in physics and 35 percent in chemistry but combined the marks to tell my mother that I got 70 percent."

The entire room erupted in laughter and there were smiles all around as I kicked off the presentation. In all likelihood, many of them thought I was joking. I was not. Those were my marks, just like the 51 percent I got the *second* time I took Grade 12 math.

Looking back now, I wonder if I actually did graduate or if they just felt sorry for me and put a stamp on the diploma based on the understanding that I would leave school and never come back. Regardless, that's exactly what I did.

•   •   •

Within days of "graduating," I headed north of Kenora, Ontario, to work for the same company my father worked for. They were building a nine-mile double-track line for the railway. This work was being completed so that trains would not have to stop and lose so much time on the side spur while waiting for the train going in the opposite direction to pass.

My dad was the mechanical superintendent on that project, meaning he was responsible for all the planning, procurement, management and operations relating to servicing and maintaining all the heavy machines and equipment for the massive project.

I believe our father had made it only to Grade 10 before having to leave school to help out on his parents' farm. When he was released from the army after World War II, he wanted to become an engineer; however, in his release documents they wrote, ". . . seek employment as a truck driver or tractor operator." Although Dad was one of the least "educated" people I've ever met, he was also likely the smartest—and certainly the wisest. While this might be the exaggeration of a loving son, I think he knew every part name and number from every heavy machine they had on the work site—by memory!

I'd had a few glimpses into Dad's career when I was younger and had the chance to spend the day with him at his work. Back then he oversaw all of the mechanics at a construction company, and it was fascinating to see him manage the shop. There were always things that needed fixing or that were in for their regularly scheduled maintenance. It was a busy place, but safety was paramount—a lesson I learned there and have followed for the rest of my life.

When I was sixteen, with a brand new driver's licence, Dad invited me to come with him to work on a large construction site in northern Quebec for the summer. It was a huge hydro project and I was excited to see it. Just before we got to Montreal, he pulled off the highway and told me that I would be driving through the city. Anyone who has driven in Montreal knows how stressful it can be, but for a rookie driver who had never operated in any city (remember, our village had around 1,100 people in it), it was truly white-knuckle time!

He was firm with his instructions, like telling me to get close enough to the car in front of me so that none of the local drivers, well-known for aggressive lane switching, could cut me off. But he was also patient and didn't get upset at me if I made a mistake. Firm but fair—another great model to aspire to.

It was frightening, but after we made it through the city with no issues, I felt good about myself and proud that my dad had the confidence in me to let me attempt the drive.

• • •

My mom had moved to northern Ontario that summer to be with my dad during this long project. I'm sure it was nice for her not to be left behind this time. With me, their youngest child, now "out of the nest," she was free to do as she pleased when it came to travelling with Dad. Over the next decade or so, they would go to both Africa and South America on major projects that Dad was hired to manage, and they even got to stop in Rome and visit the Vatican—a big deal for two devout Catholics.

I lived at the camp with all the other employees while my parents lived in a nice little cottage nearby. I would visit them on my days off and, with my first rifle, a beautiful Browning lever-action .22, would go partridge hunting. It was a nice break from the camp, where I was a child in a man's world.

The language, the surreptitious drinking (it was a dry camp) and the rowdy behaviours were all extremely new to me. I survived, but it was clear that I was a fish out of water. The fact that my dad was one of the bosses likely saved me from the worst of it, but these truly were hard men. They worked hard and played harder.

In any event, Mom was after me early in the summer to apply for university. I pushed back as much as I could, saying that there were no universities willing to accept someone with a 52 percent average. But she persisted, so I sent applications to three different universities. Of course, I was rejected by all of them. *Quelle surprise!*

Chapter 5

Constable

With university clearly not an option, I moved to Ottawa that September, in 1976, and lived with my brother, Stew, and his wife just south of the city. He helped me get a job at Beaver Lumber on Bank Street as a clerk in the hardware department. I hoped that this would be a short-term role while waiting for my application to join the Ottawa Police Force to be processed.

I was fearful that my terrible marks would be a barrier to my being hired by the police. It turned out that the bigger obstacle was the fact that I weighed only 155 pounds. Back then, there were both height (5'10") and weight (160 pounds) requirements to be hired by the police force. My solution to that problem was to eat as many bananas as I could the morning of the weigh-in. I made it, but barely. Looking back, it's been a very long time since I've seen that weight!

The application process was pretty easy, even for me. I had to answer some skill-testing questions, but nothing too difficult. It turns out that the most important questions at the time were about what kinds of sports I played. Individual sports were valued less, as it meant, to them, that you were not a team player. The fact that I played hockey, baseball (playing later for the police fastball team), basketball and volleyball meant I was a perfect fit.

Getting the acceptance letter was the proudest day of my life up to that point. For once, I wasn't a failure and I had a chance to make a difference. Maybe not like my dad did in WWII, but I could help people and be seen as successful. For someone who believed he had pretty much failed at everything before now, this was truly a new beginning. I was going to work my ass off and be successful. Everyone who had doubted me or told me I was stupid (maybe not in those words, but in their actions) would see just how well I would do.

With this mindset, I started my policing career with a huge chip on my shoulder. A chip that would grow over the years, continuously adding more and more emotional and psychological weight to my psyche.

•   •   •

I joined the Ottawa Police Force on May 16, 1977, and shipped out shortly thereafter to take what was known as "Part A" at the Ontario Police College (OPC), situated in southern Ontario, just outside the small town of Aylmer, southeast of London. Unlike some provinces, all police officers in Ontario, at least back then, had to be hired by a police force before going to OPC. (It was not until years later that most Ontario police agencies switched over to being called a "service" rather than a "force." It was almost as if removing the word would eliminate the need to use force.)

The original OPC buildings were all from when the site was a WWII Air Force base. Before the new residences were built and opened in 1975, the students had to sleep in the old military-style "H-Huts" with about thirty guys all packed in together in two rows (no women were attending OPC when I went there). The classrooms and other facilities were equally old and decrepit.

We were the second class through the recently updated college. The preceding class had had the privilege of breaking things in, so by the time we got there, everything seemed to run pretty smoothly. I arrived in my used, and very run-down, Buick to find I'd be staying in a wonderful new building with individual sleeping rooms, communal bathrooms and a "pod" that everyone shared to study and socialize. The rest of the building, including the classrooms, gym and drill hall were all beautiful—at least to this nineteen-year-old recruit.

Having lived in a construction camp the previous year, I found this environment far less stressful. There were some older guys there, as some agencies didn't send their recruits to the college for a year or two after being hired. Even my class from Ottawa had a few older guys, as they had decided later in life to join the police force. Overall, though, almost everyone there was my age or a few years older.

While it was very much a competitive environment, something that was encouraged by our instructors, everyone got along pretty well. We worked hard, studied hard, exercised hard and, on the weekends that we had to stay there, partied hard. I loved it!

• • •

For the first time in my life, I wasn't the stupidest guy in the room (although I have to say, I met no stupid guys at OPC). I excelled in every class. I can't recall what my graduating average was, but it was in the high nineties. Now, to be clear, this was not Physics 101. These were classes about the law, the use of force, powers of arrest, search and seizure and so on. All things that would have a practical application in my future career.

Yes, there was the obligatory memorizing of mundane facts that we would likely never use and could always look up in the Criminal Code or Highway Traffic Act. But I didn't mind having to remember all these details; I just relished the fact that I was doing so well. I felt like I was finally part of something. Something bigger than me and something that would lead me to years of fulfilment.

There were two activities at the college that I loved the most. First was eating. I had never seen so much food in my life, and I loved it. Some people complained about it, but I was working out and running every day and just packed in the limitless food, including nice cold chocolate milk!

By the time I left Aylmer, I no longer had to worry about meeting the minimum 160-pound requirement for being a constable. I put on a ton of weight at OPC, and it was all muscle. Not that I was a big guy; I just finally started to put on some mass.

The second thing I loved was shooting class. We used these old Smith & Wesson .38 Police Special handguns. They took six rounds of ammunition and fired in either "double-action" or "single-action." Double-action meant that you had to pull the trigger smoothly with about six pounds of pressure to pull the hammer back and then drop it forward to fire the gun. This was the primary method of shooting because, they told us, there would be no time in a gunfight for single-action. Although more accurate over longer distances, with single-action you had to manually pull the hammer back with your thumb until it locked into place in the firing position.

All of our training was designed to be as realistic as possible. According to statistics back then, and I don't think this has changed much over the years, most police shootings last less than three seconds and take place within three metres of the subject.

Stop and think about that, as I know we did when first told this. Three seconds to determine the rest of your life. This was when I learned the saying, "I'd rather be tried by twelve than carried by six." In other words, officers would rather be charged after a shooting than require a police funeral, missing the rest of their lives and leaving their grieving family behind.

Some might read that saying and be shocked, especially these days with all the anti-police sentiment so prevalent in society. I guess I would ask that you imagine the officer being a member of your family.

Everyone involved, from the police force to the college to the recruits, wanted to do the right thing. I've never met a police officer who I thought was in that role to hurt people. Were some too aggressive? Yes. Did some step over the line? Yes. Did I ever step over the line? Yes. Am I proud of it? No.

July 11, 1977, was a day I will never forget. I was studying with some other recruits in our pod when someone came in and told us that several Ottawa police officers had been shot. We all rushed to the only TV that was available to us to get the news (there was no Internet, Google or social media back then). We were shocked to learn that an officer was dead, several others had been shot and injured and dozens of police officers had been involved. We learned the next day that Constable David Kirkwood was the officer down. He was in the class just before us and had helped break in the new OPC. He was a rookie—just like us.

I still get emotional just writing this and thinking about it. Dave, whom I never met but who was friends with officers I would later become friends with, was dead. He was leaving behind a family—his wife, Dawna, who was one month pregnant with their daughter, Tricia.

This was a part of my policing career that I would never get used to. I've attended more police funerals than I care to remember. All of them, and those that I was unable to attend, are reminders of the ultimate sacrifice too many have paid while protecting Canadians across this great country.

But not all fatal wounds are physical. A shocking number of police, other first responders and members of the military bear the horrible scars of post-traumatic stress disorder (PTSD), brought on by the horrific events we have to witness in the line of duty. (Within the first responder and military communities, many prefer the term "operational stress injuries, or OSIs," or simply "injuries," recognizing the impact of service-related trauma.) Sometimes these invisible injuries are too much to endure. While it was far less heard of, and never talked about back then, the issue of suicide among the police population (as well as military personnel and other first responders) has finally now been recognized as a major tragedy in our chosen profession.

Based on my upbringing as a Catholic, I had always viewed suicide as a sin and, ultimately, as the coward's way out. While those were my general thoughts on suicide at the time, I had no idea then how personal they would become or that many years later I would almost be a statistic of that kind of tragedy.

•　•　•

I completed the basic Part A training at OPC a few weeks later and returned to Ottawa, where I was assigned to work with an experienced officer who would be what's known as my "coach officer." He worked Car 107 in the Overbrook part of Ottawa. This was not an overly busy area, not like the ByWard Market or Bank Street around the various bars near Gilmour Street in downtown Ottawa.

My coach officer was very focused on enforcing traffic-related offences, so we spent a great deal of time stopping cars and giving out tickets. It was all great to learn, but I felt jealous of other rookies whose coach officers were more focused on catching criminals. They seemed to be learning much more than I was, and I remember wishing I could get moved to a more active area.

I was only in my second week with my coach officer and we were working the afternoon shift. We received a call that, looking back, impacted the rest of my life and certainly helped me move further towards alcohol. While this has never been formally diagnosed, it also likely became the first link in my post-traumatic stress injury chain, a chain most first responders build throughout their careers and continue to carry for the rest of their lives.

It was a sudden-death call. When we arrived at the high-rise apartment block on St. Laurent just north of Montreal Road, we were directed to the rear of the building. There, we found a twenty-two-month-old child on the rear concrete deck, clearly dead.

I won't share the details with you, but I could. I could tell you every last detail. The sounds. The smell. The birds. Everything. That scene is as vivid in my mind as is the scene outside my window as I write this. It's likely even more vivid. I will never forget it.

I was left to guard the body. I couldn't stop staring. I felt sick to my stomach but didn't throw up. On a mental level, I understood what I was seeing. On an emotional level, I had no idea what to think or how to handle it.

We had received some training while at the police college about how these kinds of scenes would impact us, but nothing about how to handle them mentally or emotionally. Essentially the mantra was to "suck it up" and just deal with it.

Dealing with it meant never talking about it. I never talked to my coach officer about it and, other than relaying the facts of the case, those being that a despondent mother suffering from postpartum depression had murdered her own child, I never talked to anyone about how I was feeling.

Other than my dad. I called him later that night and told him what I saw. I figured that he had seen lots of things during the war, so he would understand.

He listened to me patiently. When I was done, he told me that I had a decision to make. I was still new in my career and there would be no shame in deciding that it was not for me. However, he said, I needed to make this decision soon. He highlighted the fact that I would be seeing much more death and tragedy in the years to come and either I was in for the long haul, or I should get out now.

I don't remember exactly what I did after that call, but I am pretty sure I got drunk. And pretended that what I had experienced didn't bother me at all. Because that's what real men do. Right?

In hindsight, I wish I'd received different responses from my coach officer and my father in those vulnerable moments and the days afterwards. Thankfully, today's first responders and military members have far more resources available to them than we had back then. We are not yet fully where we need to be when it comes to under-standing, support and treatment; however, thanks to a wide range of leaders in this field, we are moving in the right direction.

What I needed back then was someone to listen, to comfort me and to be patient as I repeatedly talked about the events of that eve-ning. I needed someone to understand and help me process what I had experienced. Mostly, I needed to know that it was OK to ask for help and to accept it from wherever I could find it.

For anyone reading this and currently struggling, sucking it up is *not* the answer!

•   •   •

The only other story I want to share from my time with a coach of-ficer—a much lighter one, I promise—was the night we responded to a 10-78 ("Officer Needs Assistance") call at Bank and Gilmour. A 10-78, sometimes called a 10-33 in police services and I've also heard it referred to as "Code 30" in the States, is the highest priority call an officer can receive. It means that another officer is in deep trouble and needs help. *Now!*

In thirty-three years of policing, I responded to only a handful of these calls and never put one out myself. I was always fortunate enough to have the extra few seconds, before things went "south," to ask for help in other ways. For example, if things were bad but the person or persons causing problems were right in front of me, I would use an ultra-calm voice when speaking on my radio, saying, "Dispatch, could I see another unit here, please?" Every cop reading this knows exactly what I'm saying. It was not the words but the tone of voice that sent a subliminal, yet clearly critical, message: *I'm in deep shit here and would like someone to come help me.*

On this particular night, I was with another coach officer because mine was away. The call came across the radio as a scream: "10-78, Bank and Gilmour!"—or so I would decipher later. Still being new on the job then, the radio often sounded like gibberish to me. I was still practising my 10-codes and phonetic alphabet (Alpha, Bravo, Charlie, etc.) that we use when spelling things to the dispatcher.

I had no idea what was said, but all of a sudden, my partner hammered the gas and we were accelerating south on St. Laurent through Ogilvie Road towards the eastbound ramp for the Queensway. Google Maps now tells me that the distance we had to travel was about 5.6 kilometres away and should, according to Google, take roughly eight minutes. I'm pretty sure we did it in less than two.

As we approached the off-ramp for Metcalfe Street, we were doing way over 100 miles per hour. I can't tell you our exact speed because my eyes, which I'm sure looked like saucers, were staring straight ahead, and my fingernails were likely embedded in the dash. I don't even think we had seatbelts on because that was not yet something cops did (we do now, both for safety and to properly tie ourselves into the seat for improved high-speed driving control).

For those of you not from Ottawa, the Metcalfe Street exit is the one right beside our new police headquarters at 474 Elgin Street (opened in 1983 by Princess Diana). This is a blind exit for any traffic heading north on Metcalfe as they are travelling underneath the Queensway. In the same way that those vehicles can't see any cars coming down the ramp, drivers heading east down the off-ramp, as we were, can't see cars driving north either.

The light for us at Metcalfe was red.

We were going, to the best of my recollection, close to 150 kilometres per hour (over 90 miles per hour).

I thought we were going to die.

We didn't (obviously). We made it to Bank and Gilmour to find about fifteen other police cars there ahead of us and the problem, whatever it was, had already been resolved.

I don't remember the rest of that shift but am pretty sure we went to Molly McGuire's pub that night. That was the pattern. A few drinks together to relax after a tough day. Then a few drinks would turn into more drinks. I often felt like crap the next day because of a hangover, but I was never late for work once and it never impacted my ability to do my job. Alcohol was not a problem. It was a way to let off steam, a release.

•   •   •

After my time with a coach officer, I went back to the police college with the rest of my class to complete Part B. This final phase involved additional training and gave us a chance to ask instructors, and our fellow recruits, about our experiences during our time with coach officers.

I continued to be "that guy" who always asked questions and wanted to know "why." I don't think my instructors appreciated my need to understand the rationale behind everything, but it didn't seem to impact my marks, as I continued to excel.

There was a bit more freedom during this phase of our training so, from time to time, we would head to St. Thomas, about twenty minutes west of us. While there was certainly some drinking, everyone was on their best behaviour, as the possibility of getting kicked out of OPC and then fired by our home police services, was very real.

We also had to contend with both the St. Thomas Police and, when driving between their city and OPC in Aylmer, the Ontario Provincial Police. We had been warned that any recruit getting stopped for speeding or other traffic-related infractions would get ticketed and reported to OPC bosses.

One of my classmates found this out for himself when he was ticketed for speeding. He thought he was going to lose his job and was hugely relieved when he received only a stern warning from college instructors, most of whom were police officers on secondment from their home police service.

Because policing was, and to a certain degree remains, a paramilitary institution, it was no surprise that we learned similar disciplines as our friends who had joined the Canadian Armed Forces. Discipline, command structure, the need to follow orders without questioning them (at least during a critical incident; limited questions could follow later, depending on the boss) and marching were all part of it.

During this phase of our training, I volunteered to be a part of the Silent Drill Team, which was to perform an intricate display of advanced marching as a focal point of our graduation ceremony. The event was coming up fast and all members of the drill team had to get up early every day to practice, learning to count every step and memorize every move in just a few weeks. I enjoyed being on the drill team, as it came with some extra privileges, and I enjoyed the camaraderie within the group. Having played team sports all my life, this was an extension of that for me.

I was very proud on graduation day to be part of the ceremony, with our team performing perfectly, in front of my parents and all the other family members and dignitaries from across Ontario.

•   •   •

After returning to Ottawa, I was assigned to B Platoon, one of three patrol platoons located at our headquarters building at 60 Waller Street (before the new headquarters building on Elgin Street). Back then, rookie officers had to walk the "beat" on foot for three to five years. Only after a couple of years on the beat did you earn the privilege to work in a patrol car at all, taking over the vehicle to relieve officers with more seniority while they took their lunch breaks.

Arriving for my very first shift on the beat, which was on midnights (the shift from midnight to eight in the morning), I walked into a room filled with around fifty to sixty police officers. The staff sergeant read my name off and said I was assigned to 15 Beat, second relief (that is, covering the second lunch hour of the shift).

Of course, I had to ask, "Where's 15 Beat?"

"Rideau Street from Sussex to King Edward," was the gruff answer.

Being a bear for punishment (in other words, unable to shut up—something I still struggle with today), I asked, "Where's Rideau Street?" and received a room full of laughter and an even sterner look from the WWII veteran staff sergeant.

An experienced constable was tasked with showing me to my beat. He took me under his wing and was kind enough to show me the two space heaters hidden inside buildings that I could use to keep warm all winter.

And thus began my policing career.

. . .

The police force I started with in 1977 was not the Ottawa Police Service of today. Now, the jurisdiction includes what used to be Gloucester, Nepean and OPP areas almost as far as Arnprior, Kemptville and Rockland. Back then, we policed only the city of Ottawa—so much smaller geographically and in population than it is today. But still, it was by far the largest police agency in Eastern Ontario.

As I said, beat officers were expected to walk the beat for up to five years. No matter the weather. We were also expected to walk to and from our beats, with exceptions made for the beats that were extremely far away from headquarters, like way down on Bank Street.

As a brand-new cop, my territory, 15 Beat, was Rideau Street from Sussex to King Edward. This was long before the Rideau Mall or most of the buildings that are there now, and it included two bars, Molly McGuire's (also known as Molly's) and the Black Swan.

The Swan was a rock bar and, not being into rock music, I don't think I ever went into the place other than for work-related duties. Molly's was a wonderful Irish pub where most of us went to drink after work or on days off. Molly's was also important because the night cleaning staff would let beat officers come in after the pub had closed to get warm and, if necessary, catch some sleep.

Now, for all the non-cops reading this, please don't get upset at me, or other cops, for sleeping on the job. There will be much more to get upset about later in the book. For now, understand that back then, before systems were put in place to improve this issue, police officers who worked afternoons or midnights also spent a great deal of time in court during normal working hours, even on our days off. While the pay was great for going to court during the day, because we were doing it in combination with our regular late shifts, it took an extremely heavy toll on us mentally and physically.

Our work schedule, negotiated by our police association (union), was designed both to maximize efficiency as well as give us as much time off as possible, but it had officers on the late shift working seven nights in a row. If my memory serves me correctly, we started nights on Friday night and finished the last night shift the following Friday morning. The shifts started at 11 p.m. and finished, if you weren't working overtime on a case, at 7 a.m.

We would often finish work at 7 a.m., go home and sleep for an hour or so and then get up, shower, put on a suit and go to court. Sometimes we were there for only a few minutes before being told that we were not needed. This was often because a deal had been struck between the assigned Crown attorney and defence lawyers, or perhaps the accused had failed to show up and a warrant had been issued, or various other reasons.

We would submit our court slips to ensure we got paid and then head back home to sleep. Or down to Molly's or the Albion Hotel (conveniently located right across from the police station and courthouse) for a beer, or two—and then home to sleep.

However, it was also very normal to be stuck in court the entire day, sometimes getting to testify at the end of the day and sometimes being told we needed to come back at some point in the future or, in a major case like a homicide, be back the next morning to start all over again. Far from efficient, I know, but I was still a constable then and had no say or influence in the matter.

We would often be operating on just a few hours of sleep, say from about 7 p.m. to 10 p.m., when we needed to get up, shave, shower and get to work without being late—a major no-no. So, after walking to the beat, checking all my doors, front and back, by 4 a.m.

I would be a walking zombie. As a result, the cleaner at Molly's was 15 Beat's best friend.

I, like almost all the officers when on the night shift, would sleep for a while on one of the benches while he cleaned. He would also keep an eye out for our sergeant, whose job it was to check on us, which was known as "pegging." (The sergeant also ensured that we followed all the rules, like not chewing gum or having our hands in our pockets while walking the beat. Both of those infractions could see you lose one or two days' pay!) The cleaner would wake us up if he saw the sergeant driving on Rideau Street, likely looking for the beat officer. We would quickly slip out the back door and walk down an alley or two, coming out much farther to the west, pretending that we had been checking to be sure the buildings there were secure—our primary responsibility.

The sergeant would then find us and ask where we had been (after all, they had been constables once too and knew the game). We would give the standard answer, "Checking doors behind these buildings, Sarge," and they would continue on their way to the next beat.

•   •   •

One thing I learned early in my career is that cops, and most first responders or members of the military, share a dark sense of humour. Things that most people would find disturbing, or at the very least in bad taste, are often found humorous by us. I'm sure there have been studies done on this, but I think most chalk it up to it being a coping mechanism for dealing with all the horrific things that those of us in these professions are witness to.

Understanding and addressing post-traumatic stress–related disorders has evolved significantly since those days, as outlined in the *Diagnostic and Statistical Manual of Mental Disorders (DSM-V)*. This shift in perspective has been shaped by lessons learned from military personnel returning from Afghanistan and additional key research and reports which examined police suicides and highlighted their relevance to all first responders. After years of denial, police suicides are now formally recognized as line-of-duty deaths—a long-overdue acknowledgment that these tragedies are often a direct consequence of the trauma officers routinely encounter in their work.

While TV and movies have become far more graphic today, and police procedural shows much more accurate, back then what we saw on the job rarely made it into the mainstream media. Even court reporters, who heard and saw far more than the public, were careful not to put too much graphic detail into their stories for fear of disturbing their viewers or readers.

Things were said at crime scenes to relieve the tension and to help get all of us through tough situations without thinking too much about what we were witnessing. This is also why letting off steam afterwards and going for a few drinks was considered normal back then; for better or for worse, it was the main way of dealing with mental stress.

One tale of dark humour was legendary with 15 and 16 Beats. I never knew if it was true, but it was often told. The story went that two officers were assigned to these beats years ago, shortly after World War II. Both were veterans and, as such, pretty used to seeing death. On one extremely cold night, in the middle of a major snowstorm, the officer on 15 Beat found a street person deceased in the snow right at the northwest corner of Rideau and King Edward. The officer checked to be sure there were no signs of foul play (i.e., homicide) and then looked around to see if anyone was nearby or watching.

You see, on extremely cold nights (anything lower than −30°C), officers were assigned what was called "double relief." This meant we got two breaks, both forty-five minutes long, instead of the traditional one-hour lunch break. So, at the start of a shift, officers walked to their beat and patrolled for a couple of hours, then they walked back to the station or took a bus there (originally a tram car), to warm up and get something to eat. They would then walk back to their beat, work a couple more hours, and then repeat the process. If for any reason you were busy with an incident when it was your time to return for first or second relief, there was a very good chance you were not going to get your break from the extreme cold that night.

So, 15 Beat, as whichever officer on that beat at the time was called, had a decision to make. Should he go to the call box (there were no portable radios until shortly before I joined) and let dispatch know? If he reported the body, he would be stuck guarding the scene for an extended period—missing at least one, if not both, of his relief periods. Or . . .

As the story goes, the officer decided to drag the body across the intersection to the north*east* corner of Rideau and King Edward. On 16 Beat's territory. *Let him deal with it*, he thought.

After walking back to the station, getting warmed up, eating something and most likely playing cards with his buddies, as was the practice, he trudged back to his beat. Once he finally made it back to King Edward, what did he find but . . .

The body was back on *his* corner!

•   •   •

I'm sorry if this story disturbs any readers. I'm trying to paint a picture of what life was like for me as a young, inexperienced, innocent police officer. Every day, I saw, heard and experienced an amazing array of new, often exciting, sometimes terrifying—and, too frequently, deeply troubling—situations.

When I joined the police, I was a country bumpkin and still very much a product of a strict Catholic upbringing. I rarely swore. I went to mass weekly and had an extremely strong moral compass. Almost every personal decision I made had some form of a "guilt" lens attached. Although I was living on my own now and no longer concerned about my mother's approval, if I did something, anything, that I thought God would not be happy with, I felt guilty. I believed, and still believe, that God could see everything I did, hear everything I said and comprehend every thought I had. This added a great deal of stress to an already stressful life, especially for a young, active male.

The only time I didn't feel guilty was when I drank. I lost my inhibitions and felt wonderfully free to do almost anything I wanted. I still had some limits, but nowhere near the limits I had when sober. Life was good. Until I woke up feeling terrible and feeling guilty, again, for what I had done the day before.

This was a pattern that would continue for years.

•   •   •

In the fall of 1979, one of my best friends from high school, who was a year behind me, invited me to visit him for a weekend at Laurentian University. Another Seaway District High School buddy and I drove up to Sudbury in my beautiful new 1979 baby blue Ford Thunderbird. The car was huge and just floated on the highway. My older Buick, purchased shortly after moving to Ottawa, had died on the side of the 401 near Halton Hills on the way to OPC Part B. (My thanks to the other recruits who saw me on the side of the highway and gave me a lift to Aylmer.)

Our starting salary in 1977 was $14,000, a breathtaking amount of money for a nineteen-year-old at that time. The salary went up every year on the anniversary of our hiring as we moved from fourth-class constable to third-class, then second-class and eventually first-class constable. Of course, my expenses also increased over the years as I settled down, bought a home and had a family. But back in 1979 with none of those obligations, I had more disposable cash than I would for decades, likely until post-retirement. Hence the snazzy new car.

So, there we were, driving up Highway 17 with a couple cases of beer in the trunk and a bunch of cash in my wallet. Things were going well in my life. However, it was about to get much better, yet much more complicated.

That Saturday night, there was a costume party we were going to. We had nothing to wear, so the three of us went to a local second-hand store and looked around. We found matching white T-shirts that were from an automobile shock-absorber company. They said, "I'm unshockable." We thought that was incredibly funny (we were already drinking). We also found some great straw cowboy hats with strings under the chin. It was the perfect outfit—or so we thought.

Remember, while I'm now a cop, I'm still this very shy young man who spends most of his time thinking about what everyone else thinks about me. Seeking self-worth from all my actions. Wanting to please my mother, my God, my bosses, my friends—likely in that order. Unless, of course, I'm drinking . . .

We go to the party and continue drinking. Then I see her. I look across the hall, and there, surrounded by a bunch of people, just like in a movie, I see this amazingly gorgeous girl with the most beautiful blue eyes that sparkle as she smiles. And she smiles all the time. She is laughing, engaged and so full of life that it seems like it is beaming from her. And those white jeans. *Wow.*

Sometime later that night, because I needed a few more drinks to get up the courage to talk to her, my friend introduced me to Lise Essiembre from Kapuskasing, Ontario (aka "Kap"). I'm not sure if it was truly love at first sight, but I will never forget the moment I saw her and how I felt looking at her. Did I mention her white jeans?

Over what was left of that weekend, and during a few other trips to Sudbury (with me making any excuse I could to go), we slowly got to know each other. I also learned that her older brother was working in Northern Ontario in various forestry-related jobs and that the rest of her family had moved to Ottawa with the intention that the four girls would go to university there. (They did all go to university, although none in Ottawa).

Lise's dad had been injured in an industrial accident at the Spruce Falls pulp and paper factory and had been receiving a disability pension for years. Her mom had owned the Kap Tasty Treat takeout restaurant, where everyone from Kap and the surrounding area came for fast food and soft ice cream.

Lise was in the physical health and education program at Laurentian University and was extremely athletic (which I could tell from the white jeans). She was on the varsity downhill skiing and curling teams. She loved to cycle, play tennis and just about every other sport. All of this just made her even more attractive to me.

We exchanged phone numbers and promised to stay in touch when she came back to Ottawa that summer. However, it was not until the following summer that things began to click, a bit, for her.

•   •   •

In the spring or summer of 1979, before having met Lise, I was getting frustrated that I had to walk the beat for up to five years before moving up in the ranks. Especially when I saw that friends who I had gone to police college with from Durham Regional Police Service (DRPS) were put straight into patrol cars after graduation and were free to do real policing—not just walk a beat, say hello to tourists on day shift and check to see if businesses were "secure" on afternoons and midnights.

I had made several arrests and given out various traffic tickets during my time on the beat, but I longed for "real" police work. That was done by officers in patrol vehicles and by detectives. I could not wait to become a detective! These frustrations were compounded by the fact that I was now living in Ottawa alone, as my oldest brother and his family had moved away and were living in Oshawa, just east of Toronto. Thinking the grass had to be greener there, I applied to join DRPS.

Back then, switching police forces was very much frowned upon. And the system didn't make it easy for you. If you wanted to join another force, you had to quit yours before applying to the other one. There is much more mobility today across police services, right across the country. But not back then.

For whatever reason, though, and I'm not quite sure why, probably because they were growing and needed to hire more officers, DRPS allowed me to apply without taking the risky step of first leaving my home service. I went through the process easily, and then it came time for my final interview with their hiring board. As I prepared for the interview, I knew the most critical question would be, "Why are you leaving Ottawa Police?"

If I told them the truth, that I was bored walking the beat and thought that DRPS was more progressive and would allow me to continue my policing journey much faster, they would not like that answer. Putting down my home agency would be seen as a negative, and I would likely be viewed as a malcontent. The best answer, if I truly wanted to get hired by them, was to say that it was because I had no family in Ottawa but did have strong family ties to the Durham Region. I was friends with a number of their officers and had heard nothing but wonderful things about the organization. All positive. Nothing negative. That was the way to get hired.

As I sat waiting for my interview, I was still not sure how I was going to answer this key question. I decided to pray about it and asked God for guidance. *Lord, please help me say the right thing and let your will be done.*

I went into the interview and told the truth. When it was over, the recruiting staff sergeant left the room with me and gave me the most incredulous look. He asked me why I had answered the way I did. I said simply, "Because it's the truth." Needless to say, I did not get hired by DRPS (they were likely all pissed off that I had wasted their time).

Weeks later, it was now winter and I was on "parade" for the midnight shift in Ottawa. Parade is what we called the meeting at the beginning of our shift where we got our assignments and the bosses read off various orders and crime bulletins that we needed to be aware of. They announced that we would be getting double relief tonight because it was extremely cold.

I was resigned to the fact that I would be stuck on the beat for another three years. However, that night, an inspector who I didn't know walked to the front of the room and asked for a volunteer to work in the Communications Centre, also known as Comm Centre, for a year. A thought hit me. *Freeze my ass off doing a job I hate, or go learn something new and stay warm?* I put up my hand and volunteered. I had no idea how pivotal that moment would be in my policing career.

In the Comm Centre a few weeks after that, still learning how to take calls and dispatch them using an old "punch card" type of system, the same inspector came into the room. He said they were looking for a volunteer to be Comm Centre's lead on a new technology project.

The police force was getting something called a Computer Aided Dispatch and Records Entry system, or CADRE. We would be dispatching via computers, and every police car would have a Mobile Digital Terminal, or MDT. We were the first police agency in Canada to get these MDTs (sorry, Vancouver, you were second).

I did not put up my hand to volunteer this time. However, we didn't have civilian members working with us yet and all the others working in the Comm Centre were very senior constables, most with decades on the job. I was, by far, the most junior person in the room. Everyone looked at me and said, "Valcour will do it."

Another pivotal moment. My lifelong love affair with technology and information management began.

The CADRE project was, by all accounts, hugely successful. I played a minor role, as I was so junior and still learning to be a police officer, let alone an expert in anything. However, I learned a great deal about computing, information management (we did not use that term back then) and mobile data sharing.

I soon became aware that not everyone was as keen on technology as I was and there was a consistent theme of officer distrust of anything new. While the majority of officers liked the idea of improved access to information, they detested the idea of having computers, or MDTs, in their police cars. They thought that management would be able to see and hear everything they did (partially true) or said (not true). They also thought that the bosses would know where they were at all times (also not true, at least not back then).

There certainly were, and are, logs of all transactions, including messages sent and received. Officers could send short text messages either directly to other MDTs or to a group of MDTs, such as all the cars in their assigned area. All the officers received training and were told that these messages would be tracked and that, if the system was used inappropriately, they would be held accountable. Over the years, a few officers and dispatchers learned this lesson the hard way, particularly with the first civilians hired, both female and male, who became party to their male-cop banter.

Although being involved in the CADRE project was very rewarding and put me on a path towards lifelong learning and my eventual area of expertise, the only real feedback I got at the time was quite negative.

I was asked to be involved in a photoshoot of the new cars and MDTs. I participated, and the photos looked good, I thought—until I was called into the inspector's office and given shit by him for not wearing my forage cap (police hat) for the photos in which I was standing beside the car. He didn't "charge" me under the Ontario Police Services Act, but it was certainly a stern warning. Another lesson learned: it's not what you do but how your bosses perceive what you do that matters.

•   •   •

I spent a year in Comm Centre, and the job was one of the most mentally demanding of my entire career. Even with computers to aid our work, on busy nights I would write quick notes about lower-priority calls just to keep up; notes that would then have to be entered into the system when I had a quiet moment. Often, I would wake up in a sweat later that night, wondering if I had failed to enter a particular call, and I'd call into Comm Centre to confirm that I had done it.

Calls with children involved were extremely demanding on everyone. I remember one night we got a call from OPP Dispatch saying that they had a sick child they were rushing to the Children's Hospital of Eastern Ontario (CHEO). The officer was approaching

Ottawa from the west, and they were looking for us to do an emergency escort. I was the dispatcher, so my clerk (each dispatcher has a clerk sitting beside them to provide support) was relaying information on where the OPP officer was while I was getting various officers to key intersections at the Alta Vista exit and all the way up Alta Vista and down Smythe to CHEO.

Everything worked perfectly and the child lived.

As I write these words, all these years later, I still get emotional recalling that night. And I had many other similar calls that still evoke similar emotions. These memories are almost like the chains that Jacob Marley wears in the Charles Dickens novel *A Christmas Carol*. In the novel, Marley confronts the book's main character, Ebenezer Scrooge, in his bedchamber at night. Marley states:

> *I wear the chain I forged in life. I made it link by link, and yard by yard; I girded it on of my own free will, and of my own free will I wore it. Is its pattern strange to you?*

While the chain links of stress, post-traumatic or not, are not forged by our own free will, they exist all the same. Every first responder, member of the military and others who work in a wide range of other professions start adding this mental weight to their psyche early in their career and, without help (even sometimes with it), the weight can eventually become unbearable.

I didn't understand then that I was slowly forging my own heavy emotional chain, or what the eventual impact was going to be.

•   •   •

A year later, I was transferred to our Information Desk. This was the area at the front of the Records Section that dealt with any walk-in complaints and people who wished to file a report. We had a wide range of duties, and I learned a tremendous amount during my year there.

The officers assigned here were either young, like me, or older officers who, for various reasons could not go back on the road. We typed the documents that were used to lay criminal charges on individuals, and we ensured that all the correct paperwork was included in the folders that were needed in court the following morning.

I loved night shifts, as it was relatively quiet. Other than charges laid by the Night Squad detectives (another role I would attain, and love, later in my career), there was lots of time to explore the massive files stored behind us. I would wander the aisles looking for the thickest files, which normally indicated a homicide or other major case. I pulled these files from the cabinet and sat and read for hours. I learned who the best detectives were, who wrote the most comprehensive reports and who did not. I learned their thought processes and investigative techniques, including interviewing and interrogations (at least what they shared on paper). This level of insight into how criminal investigations were launched, managed and successfully completed was like having a road map to future success as an investigator.

Another positive to working at the Information Desk was all the women who worked there. Unlike the Comm Centre, which was just beginning to hire female call takers and dispatchers, the Records Section was almost all women—other than their supervisors, who were all male.

We were warned about having off-duty relationships with Records staff, but for many of the other Information Desk officers, this was pretty much ignored. For me, still being extremely shy and having an overarching fear of ever doing anything that might be considered

a "sin," I was wary of getting too involved with anyone. I did go
on a few dates and went with the group when they were heading to
Molly's or over to one of the infamous bars in Hull, like JR Dallas.
Overall, though, I pretty much stayed in my little shell.

•   •   •

When Lise came back to Ottawa that summer, we started hanging out
together. I wanted the relationship to move to something more physical, but she was adamant that we be "just friends." While somewhat
frustrated over her decision, that didn't change the fact that I wanted
to spend all my time with her. Working shifts helped, as I had lots of
time off. We spent almost every day together that summer, playing
tennis, cycling, talking and drinking.

Lise was always playful and mischievous. She was also fiercely
competitive. She did not like to lose. At anything. One day we were
playing tennis and I was winning. As I walked back to serve, she
struck a ball that hit me right in the back of the head. On purpose. She
laughed so hard and thought it was funny. I felt upset, but how could
I be angry at such a wonderful, fun and giving woman? Not possible.

Another time, we were playing squash at the Ottawa Athletic
Club. I was winning (sense a trend here?) and after I scored one particularly beautiful point, Lise got upset and threw her racquet at me.
She smiled that million-watt smile and said, "Sorry, it slipped!" There
was no way she didn't throw it on purpose. She knew it, and I knew
it. I was pissed off, but how could I be angry at such a wonderful, fun
and giving woman? Not possible.

She went back to school that fall, and I continued on my journey
as an Ottawa Police officer. We stayed in touch, but she had boy-
friends and I had girlfriends. However, in my mind, none of them

would ever be able to match Lise's energy, spirit and capacity for living life to its fullest.

• • •

I returned to the Patrol Division sometime around 1981. I was now senior enough that, although I still spent most of my time on the beat, I would be assigned to a specialty car from time to time. One of these vehicles, a panel van, was known as Car 808, or the drunk tank. This van was dispatched to calls involving folks who regularly had too much to drink. Back then, they were often called "rubbies," a term that is likely offensive or not politically correct today.

The majority of times, we would pick up these people and bring them to a shelter where they would sober up, get a decent meal and then go back on the street. If they were wanted for some reason, typically a warrant for theft or for failing to pay for a meal, or if they were violent, then we brought them to the cells at the police station and lodged them for the rest of the day or night.

The first time I was assigned to Car 808, I was with a more senior officer who drove the van. I was there to assist him, as this was a two-person assignment. It was a beautiful Saturday morning in the fall and we got a call to attend Bank and Queen. When we arrived, my partner parked the vehicle up over the curb beside 240 Sparks.

A few minutes later, my partner gave me the keys and asked me to move the van to a different location. I had to back out onto Bank Street and I couldn't see well, as there were, for obvious reasons, no windows in the panel van. As I slowly backed onto the street, I felt a bump and heard this strange tearing noise. I hit the brakes, put the van in park and jumped out to see my partner staring at me in shock and disbelief. I then looked behind the van and saw a beautiful new white Cadillac—with a massive tear all along its right front fender and door! The hitch on the van had pushed into the side of their vehicle and had ripped the metal as the car drove south on Bank.

I already felt like shit, and it only got worse when two Knights of Columbus in full Fourth Degree regalia (which I recognized because my dad had the same uniform), and their wives in lovely long dresses, got out to inspect the damage. Boy, did I feel stupid. Again. We had to call a sergeant to take the accident report and, as a result, I was taken out of the rotation for any chance to drive another car for a while. I don't remember being charged or losing any pay (often a form of punishment back then), but I might well have been for such an "accident."

· · ·

The following spring, Lise told me she was going backpacking in Europe for a year with a girlfriend. I remember feeling upset and hugely disappointed, as I was looking forward to seeing her again that summer. I had thought we were getting along and that there might be something long-term developing between us, but she was adamant that she was going to take this trip. Just before they were set to leave, her girlfriend backed out. Lise left as scheduled, and I didn't see her again for over a year.

· · ·

A few months later, I began being assigned to what was called "car relief." This meant that when more senior officers, who had a regular patrol-car area assigned to them, came in for lunch, we would be assigned to replace them during their lunch hour. We would have one car area for first relief (the first lunch period) and another car area for second relief.

This was a great way to get more experience faster and to learn other parts of the city. Well, on one of my first days getting to drive a patrol car, I was dispatched to a priority call off of Bronson Avenue. It was a break and enter in progress, so priority one, meaning that I needed to get there as quickly as possible and as fast as I was allowed to.

As I approached the busy, tricky intersection of Bronson and Carling, the light was red. Ontario had just passed new regulations that prohibited emergency vehicles from driving straight through a red light, likely due to too many accidents and injuries. The rules now stipulated that we needed to come to a "full and complete stop," have emergency lights activated and siren sounding and then "proceed with lights and siren and use caution" through the intersection. (Of course, no siren when close to the scene, though, as it would scare off the burglar.) It was our job to be sure we could get through safely, and we would be responsible if there were any accidents.

I dutifully braked as I arrived at the intersection, with my emergency lights and siren activated. After coming to a full and complete stop, as witnessed by several other motorists, I hit the gas. My police vehicle made it to the middle of the intersection, where it hit the left-front side of an eastbound vehicle that was running the yellow light in the opposite direction!

Another "accident." Another sergeant called to the scene. Another way to feel stupid and be embarrassed. Not like any of the other officers would give me a hard time, right? Yeah, sure.

Police officers, and I'm sure all first responders and members of the military, love to give it to each other. An officer could make a great arrest and would certainly be praised, for a day. (Until the next day, when it would be, "What did you do for us today?") But make a mistake, say or do something stupid, the ribbing would last for what seemed like forever—sometimes for an entire career.

•   •   •

During this period, I met a lovely woman who worked at a bank on Rideau Street. I would purposely go to her till when at the bank and, eventually, I worked up the courage to ask her out. Over the next few months, the relationship flourished and we got engaged. Lise had returned to Ottawa sometime that fall and we communicated a bit, but I had moved on. It had been clear to me when she went to Europe that she had no interest in a long-term relationship.

In December 1982, our platoon had a Christmas party, as was the practice back then. Everyone got dressed up and brought their partner, in my case, my fiancée. Imagine my surprise when I walked in and saw Lise there. I was shocked and went over to ask her what she was doing at *my* Christmas party. It turned out that a mutual friend, a woman who worked in our Comm Centre, had asked if Lise would go with another officer who did not have a date.

I was so pissed off at her and, frankly, was a real jerk towards her all night long. I danced with her once and, while I don't remember what I said to her, I know it was not nice. Lise was her normal, smiling, giving, self and challenged me, asking why I was being so mean to her. Remember, I was there with my fiancée . . .

The following day, I woke up knowing I was heading to Iroquois to see my parents with my fiancée. I was quiet all day and could not stop thinking about the night before. *Why had I treated Lise the way I did? If I was marrying my fiancée, why did I care who Lise went to a party with? Why was I so upset?*

As the day progressed, it finally came to me. I loved Lise. I could not stand the thought of not spending my life with her. This posed two major problems. First, Lise was a free spirit and had zero intentions of settling down with anyone, let alone me. Second, and far more pressing, was the fact that I was engaged to a woman who, despite being wonderful, was not the woman I truly loved.

That night, after we left my parents' home, I opened up to my fiancée. It was one of the most difficult personal conversations I've ever had, but I needed to tell her the truth. I ended the engagement, and we didn't see each other again for years. Many years later, I saw her at a grocery store and we chatted. She had married and had children. I was very happy for her and wished her well.

Unfortunately, breaking off my engagement didn't seem to solve anything immediately. Lise remained fiercely independent. Having toured Europe by herself, she was now talking about working as a fitness instructor on cruise ships. She loved to travel and was extremely extroverted, unlike me, the complete introvert. She was still not interested in a long-term relationship.

I knew one thing for certain: for me to have any chance with Lise, I needed to go extremely slowly and not put any pressure on her at all. So, we remained friends, definitely without "benefits," as they say now. Not for my lack of trying from time to time, but it was not in the cards.

One trait that I possess in spades is my determination, which can be a positive or a negative. Some, possibly many, would call it stubbornness. This aspect of my personality led me to numerous successes over the years, from closing difficult criminal investigations to various other achievements, both during and after my policing career. It also often led me to take on more than I could manage effectively, and to be difficult to deal with. However, when it came to the relationship I envisioned with Lise, determination was exactly what I needed. That and a great deal of patience.

•   •   •

The world of policing is tough in many ways. We encounter so much violence, so much hatred, and see so many horrific things. It's physically demanding as well as mentally and emotionally taxing. But, as corny as it sounds, I always saw my role as a police officer as an extension of the person I am and of my personal values. For me, policing has always been an instrument for good. For peace. For good prevailing over evil. Fairness has always been a strong core value for me, and even as an inexperienced rookie, I didn't hesitate to stand up for the underdog, even during the eighteen-month probationary period when I could be fired for just about anything.

One day, I brought a prisoner into the cell block at the old police station on Waller Street. I had arrested him while walking the beat, so he was very much my prisoner. I was filling in some forms in the cell block when the prisoner, still in handcuffs, became belligerent and started mouthing off. Another constable, more senior than me by a few years, came over and hit him, telling him to shut up. I immediately pushed the officer away and told him never to do that again to one of my prisoners. The officer glared at me, told me to fuck off, and walked away. He never spoke to me again for the rest of our careers.

It was a very different time back then. Today most officers would not hesitate to report a senior officer's behaviour, plus there is video surveillance in most cell blocks and more and more cameras, both police and citizen-owned, on the street. But had I reported him then, my career would have been effectively over. The bottom line is that, at the time, I lacked both the strength and courage to do the right thing when it came to the more senior constable (although, in the moment, I did naturally protect the person in my custody). Not good, I know, but that's the way it was.

In any event, the point of me talking about how I wanted to be the protector of fairness and all things good is to say that, for the most part, when that situation took place I was still a kind, relatively soft and respectful man. Please remember this as you continue to read. Somewhere along my path, this person went missing for a long time. He was replaced by someone entirely different.

This, dear reader, is the crux of this story. Not my policing career with a few, I hope, funny stories along the way. Not even my love story with Lise. No, this story (some might call it a tragedy) is about how a nice young man from a good family, with a pretty normal upbringing changes into someone so dark, so ugly, so mean-spirited, so disrespectful and, ultimately, so broken.

So broken that he almost loses everything—including his life at his own hands.

Chapter 6
Best Friends

It was now 1983 and my policing career continued in its sixth year, with me becoming much more confident in my decision-making and the desire to move onwards and upwards. The shy kid who moved to Ottawa from Iroquois had been replaced by a self-assured young man, bordering on cocky.

Being confident and taking control of situations is critical for a police officer—or any first responder. Imagine there's an emergency and the police, firefighters and paramedics show up all asking each other what they should do! No, we need to take immediate control, make critical decisions in seconds and work quickly to resolve situations as safely as possible.

The often hidden, and very negative, side of consistently taking such decisive action is when this pattern of behaviour shifts into our personal lives. Controlling every aspect of a critical situation at work is a requirement (even more so as a duty inspector and incident commander, as I would learn years later when in charge of hundreds of major events and critical incidents). But taking the same approach with one's family, feeling a need to control every aspect of a relationship, is an extremely negative behaviour. While I was not there yet, as Lise can attest to now, there were certainly signs starting to pop up—signs that I did not recognize and Lise did not take notice of at the time.

There were also signs of my anger growing, sometimes exploding. This was especially true when she questioned a decision I had made. *Why is she questioning me? I'm an experienced cop—I know what I'm doing. What the hell does she understand about these things?*

Another aspect of the slow transformation in my personality was a growing cockiness or, put another way, a new attitude of superiority. Remember, I was the guy who had graduated from high school with a 52 percent average. I had felt stupid and inferior for most of my teenage years. Now, I was overcorrecting for my self-perceived shortcomings.

Over time, I'd learned to mask the internal dialogue of my negative self-talk. I couldn't let anyone know that I was stupid. That I didn't know what I was doing and was a fake. A fraud. An imposter. I learned that, for me, the best way to conceal these deeply held feelings was to portray the exact opposite: that I was an extremely knowledgeable and hyper-capable person. A popular saying at work was "Fake it till you make it." Normally that meant faking out suspects (or bosses). This behaviour was beginning to creep into my relationship with Lise.

As the adage goes, the best defence is a great offence (something else that I later relied on in arguments with Lise), and I was developing a growing need to show only strength and power. Anything else was weakness—and I was not weak. Or so I convinced myself and tried to convince others.

• • •

As my career developed, so did my growing friendship with Lise. She had all these funny little categories for relationships that were like doorways into the next phase of her love and affection. Looking back, I realized that they were also barriers she put up to protect herself from getting hurt. There was certainly hurt in her past, most of which I was not aware of until much later. But that's her story to tell if she ever wishes.

These categories, or barriers, had names like "special friends" and "best friends." She was open with me about what they meant to her and the fact that she would not be pressured into moving from one stage to another. It had to happen over time and naturally. I was all in and remained cognizant of the fact that I needed to be patient.

The "special friends" stage, which we had been in for a while, allowed either one of us to see other people if we wanted to. I don't think I took advantage of that option and don't know if she did—that was her business, and I needed to respect that freedom she required.

So, imagine just how happy I was in October of 1983 when Lise announced that she was ready to move to the "best friends" stage of our relationship. In a nutshell, this meant that we were no longer free to see anyone else, we were now going out with each other exclusively. This was a big deal. Lise still lived with her parents in the east end of Ottawa, right on the edge of Vanier, and she told me this as I was walking her back home down Somerset Street when we stopped at the water fountain at the top of Strathcona Park (decades later, we lived in the area and walked in that beautiful park along the Rideau River often).

I was thrilled to know that our relationship was, finally, moving on. I could not have been happier and told Lise so. A more observant person might have sensed a small lack of conviction from Lise, though, maybe better described as a kernel of fear. Not fear about me, but a fear of truly committing to one person. I did not sense this at all and was ecstatic about being Lise's best friend.

At least for about twenty-four hours.

The following day, Lise called me and said that she had made a mistake. She was not ready to make this transition and wanted to go back to being special friends. I felt hurt and disappointed. However, I knew from experience that if I pushed, I would lose her again, and likely forever. So, I agreed, and things continued as before.

A few weeks later, she once again announced that it was time to move to the best friend stage. My response when she had moved the clock backwards on our relationship was exactly what she had needed. She was really ready now. Best friends it was!

Over the coming months, we saw each other almost every day. If I wasn't at work or doing something with the guys from work, like playing hockey or golf, I was with Lise. We spoke all the time, and re-member, this was before mobile phones. We talked about everything, shared everything and truly became best friends.

I would often go to her parents' house for dinner. Their fami-ly was Francophone. Her mom came from the beautiful village of Moonbeam, just outside Kapuskasing in Northern Ontario, where there is a large Francophone community. Her dad, an Acadian from the area around Bouctouche, New Brunswick, had moved to the Kapuskasing area to work as a *bûcheron*, or lumberjack.

When I first started seeing Lise, I spoke almost no French (an-other class I had failed in high school, as I couldn't see any use for learning the language). I worked hard to get better and later took various classes through the police force and on my own at night school.

Being the kind of person who thrives on praise (maybe because of a lack of it when younger), I wanted to impress Lise's family with how well I was doing with learning French. I asked Lise to teach me a nice term of endearment, like sweetheart or something like that. We worked together to practice for a week or so until I got the accent just right. Then, at a big family dinner, I took a couple of drinks (speaking another language is much easier when you are less self-conscious) and waited for just the right moment to utter my new-found phrase.

When there was a pause in the conversation, I looked at Lise and started my sentence with "Ma belle petite crotte de nez." The room went silent and I could see Lise's family looking at her to understand what I had said. Lise said something quickly in French and then told me that they were just surprised at how good my French was. I felt proud and had a real sense of accomplishment for becoming so proficient in this wonderful new language.

Months later, I came to learn that I had said that Lise was my "beautiful little nose snot." Lise thought this was so funny, and in hindsight it was, but I certainly didn't feel very good about having called her a booger!

•   •   •

Around this time, I was finally working a regular patrol car, something I had aspired to for a long time, first in the south end of Ottawa and later in the west end. I remember one extremely hot Saturday afternoon shift, so hot that I started sweating as soon as I left my vehicle to deal with a call. We had air-conditioned cars, not for us but to help keep the MDTs cool, and it was like getting out into a furnace and then back into a fridge every thirty minutes or so.

Shortly after 6 p.m., I got a call to attend the location of a well-known pool sales and service company in the west end. There was an alarm coming from the store, likely because the employee assigned to lock up at the end of the day had failed to do so properly. Nonetheless, you can't be complacent in dealing with alarm calls and need to be vigilant on all calls for service.

Policy dictated that two officers attend all alarm calls, but I was the first to arrive (we had one officer per car then, with very few two-person cars). I checked the back door first and it was secure. I was sweating as I walked around to the front door, not because of being nervous but because of the sweltering heat, and found that it was unlocked. I advised dispatch that the building was "insecure" and entered. As there were no signs of forced entry, I was pretty confident my first inclination was correct, that someone had failed to lock up properly; but again, you can't take chances, so I was being cautious.

I checked the entire first floor and found nothing suspicious. I then walked down the stairs towards the basement and was amazed by what I saw: three beautiful, crystal clear, aqua-blue, fully operating swimming pools. I could not believe my eyes or, when I touched the water in the largest of the three, how refreshing the cool water felt.

I let dispatch know there was no need for a second officer to attend and that the building had likely not been locked properly. Dispatch told me they were unable to locate a "key holder." This meant that no one would be coming to lock the doors and I would need to ensure that I found a way to secure the building before clearing for my next call.

I stood there, hand in the water, thinking. This was one of those seminal moments in every police officer's career. I could follow the book and do everything the way policy dictated, or . . .

I walked back to my police car, sat down, and composed a message on the MDT to all the other officers in the west end. I told them not to say anything over the radio but to meet me at my location as soon as they could, park behind the building and meet me in the basement. I then went back inside, undressed and jumped in the pool.

Over the next few minutes, every officer working in the west end of Ottawa started to arrive and came down into the basement.

(We did not have GPS in the cars then, so there was no way to track where our vehicles were.) I watched as their faces transformed from puzzlement to massive smiles. One by one they, too, got undressed and jumped in the pool. (For the record, there were no female officers working in the west end that day.)

The last officer to arrive was very much a "by the book" kind of guy, but even he (likely with quite a bit of trepidation) started to unbutton his uniform shirt. However, before he got too far, the radio came to life, calling for Car 210, my car area. I didn't have my radio with me in the water, obviously, so I asked him to respond for me (our radios could not yet track who was speaking, so any officer could pretend to be another by pushing the mike and saying, "Go ahead").

The dispatcher came back over the radio and said, "We've located the owner, and they will be there in five minutes to secure the building." Well, you've never seen so many cops scrambling so fast to get the bare minimum of clothing onto their soaking-wet bodies and hustle up the stairs and out the door to their cars to peel out of there.

I looked at the last officer to arrive, with his nice dry hair, and pleaded with him to deal with the owner when he arrived. If our sergeant found out about this, we would all be in deep shit, especially me as the ringleader. He didn't want to do it, but he said he would stay. I ran up the stairs, still holding my vest and duty belt in my hands, got into my car and left as quickly as I could.

I was scared to death that I was going to be in big trouble and expected that terrible call to come from dispatch saying, "10-19 the station to see the inspector." However, a few minutes later, the officer who had stayed behind pulled his police car in beside mine, with him facing one way and me the other (it's much easier to talk this way when your car is your office, and it's often done when a sergeant needs to have a short meeting with one of their officers).

He told me that the owner had arrived and walked around the first floor with him, saying that everything looked fine. The officer had tried to convince the owner that there was no need to go down into the basement, as everything was secure. However, the owner wanted to be sure and walked down the stairs. He saw all the water on the floor and wet footprints everywhere. He watched the officer look down sheepishly and give a half-smile indicating "busted," silently telegraphing that he knew his career, and ours, were in the owner's hands.

The owner thought for a second, smiled and said, "Well, officer, I guess everything is in order here, right?" The officer responded saying, "Yes, sir." The owner told the officer he could go and that he would lock up in a few minutes.

I've wanted to write that story for decades and have told it many times to the great amusement of friends and family. As with the rest of the book, no names are being shared here—but I'm pretty sure the Limitation of Actions (known in the United States as the Statute of Limitations) is long past for any of us to get charged under the Police Services Act.

Thankfully.

•   •   •

Alcohol continued to play a role in my life, as it does with most people at that age and stage. Lise and I enjoyed drinking together and, from time to time, we would certainly over-imbibe. The difference between the two of us (as I was to learn much later) was the reason *why* we each drank. Like most "normal" people, Lise drank to have fun and to enjoy herself. I drank because I deserved it. I deserved it because I had worked hard that week, or because my boss had slighted me, or various other reasons that I came up with.

To be clear, I was never one to drink every day. It was mostly on days off or weekends. However, when I did drink, I almost always got drunk. The idea of drinking one or two beers was incomprehensible to me. In my mind, if you're going to drink, then drink! The trouble was, I didn't always think about the consequences while I was indulging. Just as it had when I was a kid in high school, alcohol made me feel free; relaxed; included in the group. So, I went all in and forgot about everything else.

Like when Pope John Paul II visited Ottawa in September of 1984. He arrived on a Wednesday and there was heavy security for his visit. He had been shot in 1981, so everything that could be done to protect him was done. I wasn't involved in the security effort, as our platoon was on midnights. Being Catholic, though, I was expected to go to the mass being said by the Pope in the LeBreton Flats area of Ottawa with Lise and her family on Thursday morning.

I'm guessing we must've had a tough shift that Wednesday night because, as was often our practice after tough shifts, many of us went drinking at a famous watering hole in Hull right after our shift ended in the early morning. Bars like this were great because they served quarts of beer with their inexpensive breakfast. I ended up at a friend's house in Hull where we continued to drink and play poker, just the two of us. After hours of drinking and playing cards, he owed me $125. We decided to play one more hand, double or nothing. If he won, he owed me nothing. If I won, he owed me $250.

I won.

He refused to give up. "Go again," he said.

I won.

"Again," he reiterated.

I won.

He now owed me $1,000. He was so pissed off at me that he kicked me out of his house and told me to go home, which I did. Drunk.

Lise was extremely upset at me. For missing the mass with the Pope. For letting her and her family down, especially her mom who was a very devout Catholic. For winning so much money from a friend. And for drinking and driving.

She made me call my buddy to say that I was not going to take the money, something I did not want to do because I came from the school of gambling that said if you can't afford to lose it, don't play. My friend said he would take Lise and me out for a very nice dinner to pay me back, which he did (and I drank as much booze as possible on his tab).

All was good again. For now.

•   •   •

My relationship with Lise continued to grow and deepen, and now we spoke regularly about what our future would look like. How many children (five)? Where would we live (somewhere on the water)? How many people did we want at the wedding (small)? While we talked about these kinds of long-term questions, I still recognized that she might not be ready to settle down. Be that as it may, I also knew that, at twenty-seven, I wasn't getting any younger. It was 1984, my career in policing was going well and, based on feedback from my bosses, there was a good chance I would be transferred to a specialty squad sometime over the next year or so.

With all this in mind, I decided that it was time to pop the big question. I put a great deal of time and effort into the planning. Everything from getting the right ring to selecting when, where and how I would ask Lise to marry me. Our first anniversary of becoming "best friends" was October 25, 1984, so I figured that was the best day to get engaged.

That week, I invited Lise to go to our favourite restaurant for dinner to celebrate our anniversary. Late on the afternoon of our date, I went over to her parents' place a bit earlier than normal. After some polite conversation with her parents, I asked her dad if he could take a look at something wrong with my car. We went outside, and I opened the hood to make it look like we were talking about the vehicle. I then proceeded to ask him for Lise's hand in marriage. I know this is very old-fashioned and some people reading this might even feel it's inappropriate, as if he "owned" his daughter. However, both of our families were traditional and Catholic. To me, it was the proper thing to do.

He seemed genuinely happy and said he would be pleased to have me as a member of their family. We went back inside to wait for Lise to get ready. A few minutes later, her dad said he had forgotten something about my car and asked if we could look at it again. We went back outside and I opened the hood again, wondering what he was going to say. He gave me a look of concern and said, "I'm happy for you to ask her, but don't be surprised if she says no."

Are you shitting me? This was the first thing that popped into my mind. Talk about losing your confidence!

After Lise was ready, we drove to La Maison, a small, yet beautiful, French restaurant on Nepean Street. As was our practice, we had a drink before even opening the menu. Our dinners together would often take two or three hours, as we always had so much to talk about.

When the main course was finished, the waiter, whom I had met with earlier in the day to plan everything, came to the table with the dessert menus and took our orders for specialty coffees (another tradition). I asked if we could go for a short walk before he served us the next course. While allowing patrons to leave before paying was not normal, I had already cleared it with the manager (of course, Lise did not know that), so the waiter said, "Of course, Mr. Valcour." Lise was happily living in the moment and didn't seem to think our going for a walk was strange. At least, if she did, she didn't say anything.

We returned a few minutes later, and the dessert and drinks were waiting for us. Lise's back was to the kitchen, so she was the only person in the restaurant who didn't see the waiter walking towards us with a huge smile on his face and carrying a dozen red roses. When Lise saw the flowers, she looked at me with her beautiful smile and started crying. She loves roses and was both surprised and extremely happy.

Lise thought the evening was almost done, so when the process repeated itself, this time with a small jewellery box on a silver platter being delivered to me, she was, I think it is fair to say, in shock. The entire room, which was already quiet (one of the reasons we loved the restaurant), went silent. I could sense that everyone in the restaurant was looking at us, but I had eyes only for Lise. I was as excited and as nervous as I had ever been.

Remember, I had known this beautiful woman, this free spirit, for over five years now. She had always resisted, or even fought fiercely against, the idea of being held back from doing whatever she wanted. Not in a spoiled or selfish way, but in a beautiful way, much like a bird soaring in the air, free to follow its path, flowing with the winds of time and living life to its fullest every moment of every day.

It was with huge relief and even greater happiness that I heard Lise say, "Yes." There were more tears and lots more to talk about as we continued our evening, but the future was set. We would be husband and wife.

How could I ever know that such joy and excitement would turn, in just a few years, to depression and despair? How could I know that the union God was about to bless, I would tear asunder? How could I predict then how terribly I would treat my very best friend? And how could I know just how black my thinking would become and what actions it would drive me towards?

Chapter 7
Married Bliss

The year that followed was a busy one, with work going well as the planning for our 1985 wedding kicked into high gear. I continued to work car areas in the far west end of Ottawa, butting up against what used to be the City of Nepean. We had lots of fun and had a good platoon that was always there to back each other up. We made lots of arrests for a wide range of criminal activity, including robberies and break and enters.

Lise and I decided we would rather spend what little money we had on a nice honeymoon than on a large wedding. We wanted to get married in October, around the same time of year that we were engaged, and then go on a two-week cruise in the Caribbean for the honeymoon.

My parents thought we were crazy for wanting to go on a cruise. When we kids were younger, our family went to Florida several times. One of those times our dad, after being begged by Stew, took us deep-sea fishing. Stew caught a massive sailfish, but I was seasick the entire time! Regardless, Lise and I wanted to do the cruise and were assured by my brother Gary's wife, who worked at a travel agency, that these ships were large and stable. Although we might feel a bit seasick the first day, we would be fine, she told us.

The cruise we wanted to take left from Florida on Sunday, October 27. That meant Lise and I needed to get married on the same day we were engaged, October 25, which turned out to be a Friday in 1985. Some may have thought it odd that we were getting married on a Friday; however, this was the only way we could make it to Florida to board the cruise ship on time.

It was a beautiful ceremony, held at Lise's family parish, Notre Dame de Lourdes, on Montreal Road. Everything went well and we even had the Ottawa Police Choir sing. Lise looked gorgeous and radiated such a beautiful smile and energy. It was the happiest day of both our young lives, and we could not wait for our journey together to begin.

The honeymoon was unbelievable. We felt a bit queasy the first night from the boat rocking, but after that it was beautiful. We loved cruising, and this would turn out to be the first of many cruises we would take. The food was amazing, the entertainment great and all the ports stunning. We loved every minute of it!

A week after we returned, we held a reception at a community hall near Lise's parents' home. While our wedding was very small, attended by just our families and those who stood for us, this was much larger and a ton of fun. We were very happy to have planned everything this way; with the honeymoon already over, we were now able to truly enjoy the reception, not having to worry about making it to the ship on time.

We purchased a nice half-plex (a wholly owned half of a duplex) in Aylmer, Quebec, with me getting our down payment by selling the house I had purchased a few years earlier. In hindsight, we should have kept that house and rented it as an investment.

Money had never been a major motivator for me, likely because I always had some. When I was growing up, our family was far from rich, but my parents certainly provided well for us. I remember one Christmas we got a new snowmobile; new to us, anyway. It was heavy and slow, but it sure was fun—until I got it stuck in a snow bank and wasn't strong enough to pull it out, so my dad had to come get it out for me.

Now that I was a first-class constable, I was making extremely good money. And with Lise working for a branch of the government, we could afford our home, car and entertainment expenses with no great challenge. Having said that, we did have dreams about doing even better financially, getting a bigger house for when kids arrived and being able to travel the world. All were things we discussed regularly. We certainly had the odd argument about the normal things related to married life, but finances were not, at that time, causing us any stress.

I remember our first meal together in our new home, with Lise saying she was going to cook me something nice. Now, you need to know that her mother was a fantastic cook. Dinners at their home always meant a wonderful feast, often with homemade bread (which she taught me how to make) or buns. I was busy doing something when Lise came to me in tears. She asked how I would like potato chips and ice cream for dinner, as she had not taken the steaks out of the freezer, so they were still frozen. We laughed, enjoyed our first meal and all was good (she later became a great cook).

•   •   •

One of the reasons we moved to Aylmer was the lack of traffic for my daily commute. Morning and evening traffic jams were infamous between Ontario and Quebec, with the Island Park Bridge still being only two lanes (there is now a third lane that changes between northbound and southbound depending on the time of day), but that was irrelevant to me, as I was working mostly night shifts. Well, of course, I was transferred to a straight day-shift job early in November 1985. This now meant fighting the traffic both ways every day. It was certainly not ideal, but I was looking forward to this next chapter in my policing career.

The Crime Prevention Section I was assigned to wasn't a large operation, but it was very busy and staffed with some excellent officers. We set up Neighbourhood Watch groups around the city, proudly getting our pictures taken with community members when their neighbourhood hit a certain threshold of membership, and we put up signs at the entrance to those neighbourhoods.

We also spoke at high schools on a range of topics, so public speaking was something we needed to be trained on. Fortunately, there was a great course at the Canadian Police College, located at the end of St. Laurent Boulevard, that we were all sent on. This was my first specialty course, and I loved it. Before that, I didn't enjoy public speaking, like most. Also like most, it scared the crap out of me. Especially as an introverted, shy kid from the boonies. However, the instructors were great and taught us lots of tips on how to present more professionally. I also enrolled myself in Toastmasters to further help reduce my fear and to continue improving my skills in this area. I learned much later in life that Stephen Covey, author of *The 7 Habits of Highly Effective People,* calls this "sharpening the saw."

My desire to be seen as excellent in everything I did drove me to improve. When I wasn't good at something, I worked my butt off to get better. A great quality to be sure, but like many things, it had a dark side. *What happens when I look bad? What if someone close to me does something that I perceive is embarrassing? How will it reflect on me?* With my internal demons beginning to grow, not well was the answer.

In any event, I loved my time in this office, even if we rarely did traditional police work.

. . .

I was working on December 31, 1985, a couple of months after marrying Lise, and driving to a meeting in the west end when a call came over the radio that I will never forget: "All units, 10-42 [robbery] in progress at Hampton Park Plaza at the corner of Carling and Kirkwood. Two Brinks guards have just been shot. All units responding, please advise."

I was only a few blocks away and immediately responded that I was on the way. I was driving one of the Crime Prevention compact cars, but I was in uniform and wearing my bullet-resistant vest and all my use-of-force options, including our old .38 Smith & Wesson Police Special six-shot firearm.

These kinds of armoured-car robberies were happening fairly frequently back then, with the suspects often coming from Quebec. I remembered a briefing we had received from a detective on our Intelligence Squad when I was still on platoon. He told us that sophisticated robbers would often take two right turns when leaving the scene of a crime because right turns were faster with no need to wait for oncoming traffic to pass from the other direction.

I was driving south on Kirkwood towards the robbery, so, recalling that intelligence briefing, I thought the suspects, who were in a large white commercial van with some kind of dry-cleaning company name on the side, would have turned right, or north, on Kirkwood, then right again on the first street they came to. So, I turned onto the same street I thought they might have used in their escape. At the end of this street was a slight left turn down into a housing complex.

I followed the road into the complex and, sure enough, there was the white commercial van with a dry-cleaning company name on the side. I had located the getaway vehicle within a minute or so of the call going out.

My heart rate was through the roof as I tried to let dispatch know where I was and that I had located the vehicle, not knowing if the suspects were still inside. I positioned myself behind the engine block of my small car to give myself cover, and I pointed my little .38 right at the back doors of the van. However, I had two problems. First was that the officer who had been at the scene of the shooting was all amped up and not following proper radio protocol. He was continually talking and not taking any breaks, either to allow the dispatcher to share more information or for other responding officers, like me, to say anything. Information like where the suspect vehicle was now located.

The second problem was much larger. In my excitement to try and find the suspect vehicle, I had forgotten a critical lesson they drilled into us at police college: always know where you are! Well, I hadn't looked at the street sign and I had never worked in this part of the city before. I had no idea what the street I had turned onto was called!

Once I was able to get some air time on the radio, I advised the dispatcher that I had found the vehicle but that I wasn't sure of the street name. I described where I was, and thankfully it took only a few seconds for an officer from the area to identify it as Buell Street. Within seconds, there were several other officers on scene, and we quickly agreed that I would open the back door of the van while they provided me with cover.

The van was empty. The suspects were gone.

The detectives arrested the suspects later that night in Hull. It turns out that a Neighbourhood Watch had been set up in the area recently by one of the other Crime Prevention Officers. A member of the watch had seen two men park a car in front of his house and walk away carrying a heavy pillowcase (the guns). He called this in, and an area car came and ran the vehicle's plates. The parked car was not stolen and there were no flags on the national computer system, so the officer cleared from the call.

Right after the robbery, the same officer drove back to find the suspicious car and, of course, it was gone. This was about a block from where the getaway van had been dumped, so it was clear that the suspects had walked from the van to their second getaway car, actually owned by one of them, to drive away from the scene.

Once the detectives were made aware of the call from the Neighbourhood Watch witness and got the licence plate from the officer who had taken the original call, it took only a matter of hours for them to identify the suspects. They located and arrested the three of them later that night (two who had been in the car that was dropped off and one who had been driving the white van).

Back at the scene of the white van, I had another problem. For whatever reason, and this never happened again in my career, I didn't have my duty book. (I became hypervigilant about this *and* about knowing exactly where I was for the next thirty years.) Our duty books are small notebooks with numbered pages that we write all our notes in. We were taught to write on every line, using a specific way to end each entry and start the notes for the next day, so we could prove in court we didn't go back and add something later.

When testifying in court, we would ask if we could refer to our notes. We would be asked if the notes were made by us (Yes), if there were any additions or deletions made after the fact (No), and if we had referred to the notes while preparing to give testimony (Yes). Typically, we were then allowed to pull out the notebook and refresh our memory with specifics from the case, as there could be pages of notes in complex investigations.

I didn't have a notebook to record my actions and observations in. The only thing I could find was an envelope from a love letter Lise had sent me, which I happened to have in one of my jacket pockets. I proceeded to write reams of notes, as small as possible, and draft a drawing of the scene to show how I had found the van. My notes were all over the envelope and at multiple angles. It looked terrible, but that was all I had. I just prayed that I would never have to testify in court.

No such luck!

A couple years later, I was called to testify in this case and take the stand. I didn't need to refer to my notes during the examination by the Crown attorney. However, when the defence lawyer began his cross-examination, he immediately asked if I had referred to my notes when preparing to give testimony. I hesitantly said I had. I think he thought he had caught me in some kind of a lie because you could see him perk up and continue asking the standard questions about my note-taking. I could tell he couldn't wait to see the notes. He was, I believe, convinced there was something in there that he could use against me and for the benefit of his client.

Eventually, he asked to see the notes. Slowly, I pulled out my notebook from that period and then, to his surprise, and the surprise of the Crown attorney and judge, I pulled out the old envelope with notes scribbled everywhere, which I had inserted into my notebook, held in place with elastics. I explained that I had forgotten my notebook that day and the envelope was all I'd had to write on.

He took the envelope, looked at it closely, turning it around in his hands. He looked at the judge, who said something about there being no doubt that these notes were the original (who the hell would make up a stupid story like this, appeared to be the subtext of his comment).

I gave a nervous smile and was massively relieved when the lawyer said, "No further questions for this witness, Your Honour."

The three accused, who were all on parole at the time of the robbery for similar crimes, later pled guilty and received lengthy sentences, the longest being twelve years in penitentiary.

This case solidified something I had known since working at the Information Desk and reading all the major case files. I wanted to be a detective.

•   •   •

My time in the Crime Prevention Section also introduced me to two new skills that I would learn to love: research and writing. We've already established that I was far from a good student in school. However, two classes I did enjoy were English and history. I loved (and still love) to read, and I did so at every opportunity. I'm certain this was, unconsciously, part of my drive to be seen as smart or intelligent. But it was also something I very much enjoyed.

While working one day, I came across a film (the old kind in a canister that you loaded onto a projector) called *The Kids' Case Against Vandalism*, which was about a student who committed vandalism at school and various kids had to play different roles in the case against him. One of the kids was the accused, others were the Crown and defence attorneys, one was the judge, others were witnesses and the remainder of the class were all part of the jury. The case went to "trial" and, in the end, the "jury" had to discuss the pros and cons of finding the "accused" either guilty or not guilty.

I thought it was a great way to engage teenagers in both a legal and moral discussion about the rights and wrongs of committing a crime (albeit, at least in their minds, a relatively minor one). I researched the film, found out as much as I could about the initiative and then wrote a proposal for our staff sergeant, asking for permission to create a program based on the premise of the film in local high schools.

The project was approved, and I soon began running similar re-enactments in interested schools. It was great fun for everyone, and many of the students got right into it—with some pretty heated debates occurring when it came time for the "jury" to deliberate on what their decision would be. My role was to help facilitate the mock trial, answer questions about the law and, with much help from the teachers, keep things somewhat orderly.

After running the program for a few months, I took the opportunity to write about it and had the article, titled "Kids' Case Against Vandalism" published in a 1985 issue of the RCMP *Gazette*, which is read across Canada and around the world.

This recognition certainly helped to stroke my growing ego and got me noticed by some of the bosses.

• • •

Married life continued to be wonderful. Lise and I loved going out together and hanging out with friends. We went to all the work-related parties and even joined a mixed slow-pitch team with other police officers and their spouses. Alcohol was almost always present, but it never seemed to be a problem. At least not that anyone could see.

I found ways to get a few extra drinks in during social events and always made sure to buy enough to last, even taking the extra step to ensure there was some booze that only I had access to. At home, I loved to barbeque our meals because I could stand outside cooking and have an extra beverage or two, unnoticed. When Lise went to bed, I would tell her I was going to stay up for a while to watch TV. That's when I would open the Grand Marnier, or whatever "reward" I had set aside for myself. Mentally, I could always justify this extra drinking because I "deserved" it.

I was still not drinking every day. I would go for weeks without getting drunk. As a "binge" drinker, it wasn't the frequency of my drinking that was the problem; the issue continued to be the underlying reason *why* I was drinking and, now, what it was beginning to do to me and our marriage.

I'm sure that some people are reading this and thinking that the kind of drinking I was doing is normal. Some of you might drink like this yourself. In all likelihood, you don't have an issue with alcohol. You are likely a "normal" person who drinks from time to time and gets drunk infrequently. If that's the case, then you likely don't have any issues to worry about.

For me, though, I have never been able to understand the concept of having just a couple of drinks. While I was able to do it in certain settings, I didn't understand it. I still thought, if you're going to drink, then drink! I drank to get drunk. All my problems went away when I drank. I didn't feel stressed about getting ahead at work. Money, which was beginning to get a bit tight, was not a concern.

Typically, I would wake up the next day with a hangover, feeling guilty. *Why did I drink so much again last night? Why was I so mean to Lise?* These were all warning signals that, unfortunately, were invisible to me. It was like the clues were everywhere, but I didn't have the special glasses (that is, the education or understanding) required to see them. Frankly, even if I had seen the signs, like all the guilt I was beginning to feel, I likely would have ignored them. *I don't have a problem. I can stop any time I want. And, anyway, it's not like I'm an alcoholic. They're the people I pick up off the street when I walk the beat or drive the drunk tank.*

Right?

• • •

We were enjoying my being on the day shift, and Lise happily took advantage of the great cycling paths in the National Capital Region to bike to work every day in the summer. However, the commute in heavy traffic was wearing me down. I couldn't see making these lengthy drives every day for the rest of my career. We were also beginning to discuss having our first child. For various reasons, primarily health care, we wanted our kids to be born in Ontario. So, we began looking for a place to live in Ottawa, where the cost of housing was, and continues to be, significantly higher than in Western Quebec.

We were able to find a cute little bungalow in the south end of Ottawa, off of St. Laurent near Pleasant Park. It was situated between a couple of low-income housing projects, but the street was nice and quiet, and we had a lovely little backyard that our future kids could play in. The house was very small, around nine hundred square feet, but the basement was finished and even had a bedroom that we could rent out if we wanted. The kitchen was so small it was hard for the two of us to be in there at the same time. I wasn't sure that this was a great investment, but Lise, who could always see the potential in things, was convinced that it would be perfect.

At the very least, there would be no more fighting traffic every day for me!

• • •

A few months later, I was happy to learn that I was being transferred to the General Assignment Section of our Criminal Investigations Division. I was now a detective, sometimes jokingly referred to as a "BCI," or big city investigator. This also meant going back to shift work. I found it ironic that shortly after buying in Quebec I was transferred to straight days, and shortly after moving back to Ottawa I was back on shifts. As the old saying goes, "Man plans, God laughs."

Being a detective was nowhere near as glamorous as I thought it would be. My first case was to investigate a man who was allegedly keeping too many pigeons, an offence under the city's animal bylaw. I quickly graduated to slightly more interesting crimes like bicycle thefts and vandalism, but they were still fairly low-priority in my eyes.

While money had never been very important to me, I loved the extra cash that I was now earning due to overtime. As a detective, this happened regularly—for example, when I had a case that required extra investigative time or if the accused was being held overnight for a bail hearing in the morning. After a few months of working these cases, the extra pay for also going to court as the investigator started to kick in as well.

One of the other great advantages to being an investigator was the fact that we were the Crown attorney's key assistant during court preparation and trial. No longer was I relegated to sit outside the court for days on end wondering when I might be called to testify or how the trial was going. In the past, I might have made the initial arrest as a patrol officer, but the person in charge, at least from the police perspective, is the lead investigator.

This role continued to support my ever-growing ego and my desire and ability to control the events I was involved in (as much as they could be controlled within the justice system). How I was viewed by my peers and those with whom I came in contact was also becoming increasingly important to me. Anything, and I mean anything, that might make me look bad, or worse—stupid or ill-informed—caused me to have an extremely strong reaction.

I recall one such instance when one of my bosses wrote something negative about me in a quarterly assessment. I don't even remember what the issue was, but I do remember writing a three-page rebuttal to this perceived slight. I even took a copy to human resources and demanded that it be attached to my file. In hindsight, this reaction was totally over the top and likely caused a great deal of discussion among other managers. As I would later learn when I was a boss, or when coaching minor hockey, no one needs the hassle of having someone who is temperamental and arrogant on their team.

In my mind, though, I was fighting for one of my core values: justice. When I perceived that I was being treated unfairly, I reacted strongly. The good news was that I felt the same way when others were treated this way and was compelled to stand up for them or protect them—likely one of the reasons I became a police officer. The bad news was that when it was happening to me, I didn't seem to have normal filters to help me turn down my reaction, particularly when I was in private, like at home.

Overall, though, I loved being a detective. Other than that secretive group that worked in the Intelligence Section (we mere detectives couldn't even get into their office), this was where things happened.

I remember one day when the staff sergeant, one of the most respected cops I've ever had the pleasure of working with, came into the office and called us all together. He introduced an investigator from the RCMP who told us an extortion was about to take place, in one hour, at the Château Laurier Hotel.

Our staff sergeant barked out orders like a military commander, with everyone jumping to complete their assignment in record time. I was tasked with going to the property room and getting a couple of suitcases to make myself look like a hotel guest waiting to get into my room. I ran to the property room, quickly explained what I needed, signed for the bags (everything gets signed in and out) and ran to the unmarked police car waiting for me at the front of the station. Within about twenty minutes of getting my orders, I was sitting in the side lobby at the Château Laurier with a picture of our suspect in my pocket, waiting for the show to start.

As it happened, the suspect, his partner and the victim all sat directly behind me about thirty minutes later. I could hear almost everything they were saying, and it was abundantly clear to me what would happen to the victim if they did not sell the suspect their property for the massively below-market value being offered.

This was not like on TV where the good guys swooped in at the end of the scene and arrested everyone on the spot. No, they all left after the meeting, and I spent hours writing notes that were as detailed as possible and then typing my report. I don't believe that the suspect was ever charged for this particular crime, but I do know that he was eventually jailed for an extended period for a series of murders. Who knows the total amount of damage he caused various families in our region?

As was the practice, everyone—detectives and criminals alike—went out that night to drink at the Prescott Hotel on Preston Street. I learned that this was the regular haunt for both camps and that it was like an unofficial demilitarized zone with a long-standing unwritten agreement in place to leave each other alone. Some of Ottawa's most well-known criminals and iconic detectives (I was not in that category) sat within feet of each other, all having a good time. Many of these folks grew up with each other in Ottawa's toughest neighbourhoods. At a certain point, they'd made a decision: Do they become a cop or a crook?

There was, for the most part, an honour system between the two sides back then: Cops are meant to catch crooks. If the crooks got caught, they gave up and paid the price. And the cops doing the catching did it fairly and without any bullshit. No mistreating anyone, and no demeaning talk or lectures. Both sides decided to live their lives a certain way, and each side "respected" the other's decisions. (This was, of course, not the case for crimes like sexual assault or anything to do with children. For those criminals, there were different rules, according to both the cops and regular crooks.)

In any event, we spent a lot of time drinking and socializing at the Prescott, which still makes the best square pizza in Ottawa!

•   •   •

A few months later, around 1986, I was assigned to Night Patrol, a small investigative team that worked straight midnights. It was a fantastic training ground for new detectives as, for major cases at least, we partnered with a seasoned investigator and worked the initial phases of all kinds of cases. This was before Ottawa Police had the numerous specialty investigative teams that they, and most major police services, have today. There were no major crime (homicide/robbery), sexual assault or spousal assault teams to be called out in the middle of the night. We took all those calls and were tasked with ensuring that the investigations got off on the right path.

There were three additional benefits to working on this detail. First was the overtime. We got tons of it, as we would work all night, brief the team(s) that were assigned the following morning and then complete our paperwork. This often added hours to the night and ensured a steady flow of additional pay. The second benefit was the fact that any time we had to go to court on our cases, it was on a day off. That meant we were getting extra pay every time we went to court, even if it was only for a few hours.

The final benefit, at least in my mind, was that we weren't assigned any cases for ongoing follow-up. We worked a case for a few hours and then handed it over to another investigator for the long-term investigative process that can take days, weeks, months or even years in some cases. We worked a case, handed it over in the morning and went home. Almost always.

One night, I had a complex case handed to me by the sergeant who did the nightly assignments. I don't even remember the details, but I worked hard all night and formed the opinion, for whatever reason, that I needed to keep working during the day shift. I did not want to let it go. While following through like this was not normal practice, it did happen from time to time. I went to see the day-shift staff sergeant and pretty much demanded to keep working the file (and get paid overtime to do it). I put it to him in similarly bold terms, and he probably didn't like my approach, so he said no.

Now, this particular boss had an outstanding investigative background. Years of experience versus my minute amount. He was also known to be volatile. None of that mattered to me, in my heightened state of ego and self-worth. We argued, loudly, with the door to his office wide open for everyone to hear. I remember looking out and seeing all the other investigators leaving—none of them wanted to be a witness if this went further south.

I felt that I was fighting an injustice—to me—and, truth be told, I wanted the extra money. He was doing what his experience told him to do. And who knows, maybe the bosses had been instructed to cut back on overtime and he was just doing what he was told.

He ended up letting me work the case for the rest of the day, so I felt victorious in my argument. What I didn't have the emotional intelligence to see at the time was that I had just hurt an important relationship and embarrassed a seasoned officer, all for my gain. I was completely blind to any of that.

In my mind, I only understood that I was being questioned and told I couldn't do something that I believed was in the best interest of the police force. It was a "win at any cost" fight for me, and this was becoming my standard operating procedure, both at work and, slowly, at home.

• • •

A few weeks later, I was called into the inspector's office. Typically, this is not a good sign. While it could mean a few positive things, it was often a precursor to bad things, like being sent back to patrol. With my very public argument still fresh in my mind, I was ready to defend my position. I asked the inspector if he was calling me in to talk about the altercation. He said, "If I wanted to talk to you about that, you would have been in here that day."

He proceeded to tell me that I was being transferred to the Enforcement Squad, a group of eight investigators made up of four sergeants and four detectives (constables, like me, who were assigned to the Criminal Investigation Division and got some extra salary to pay for things like suits and dry cleaning). The team, one of the few specialty investigative teams at the Ottawa Police, focused on four major kinds of cases—liquor, gambling, pornography and prostitution—and was led by a staff sergeant. This kind of team was often called the Morality Squad in other cities.

I didn't know a great deal about the team or what they did, except that they regularly worked undercover to arrest prostitutes. I didn't consider this to be real, long-term undercover work like the drug squad or major crimes investigators did, going undercover for long periods. This was just pretending to be "johns" looking for a prostitute.

I thanked the inspector but told him I was not interested in working on this team. I explained that I was still in the honeymoon phase of our young marriage and that my "picking up" hookers regularly was likely not going to go over too well with my new bride. I started to share a few other concerns I had, but he cut me off, telling me I had two options: take the transfer or go back to uniform duty on a platoon. It was clear that I had no choice. It was also apparent that while he had never called me in to give me shit over my argument with the staff sergeant, he was not willing to put up with any bullshit from this rookie investigator. I took the transfer.

I went home that night and told Lise about the discussion and that I had pushed back about taking the job. I explained, to the best of my knowledge at the time, what kinds of duties I would be doing, including arresting prostitutes. Of course, Lise was concerned, not about anything to do with the prostitutes but about my safety. She knew that anytime police officers come in close contact with the kinds of people we deal with daily, there is a risk of getting injured. Overall, though, as was almost always the case, she was supportive and tried to help me put a positive spin on the transfer.

It turned out that being transferred to the Enforcement Squad was one of the best things ever to happen to me during my career. There were great guys on the team, and my partner, who was a sergeant, had a ton of experience, so I learned a great deal from him. The staff sergeant was also super, a real family man, and he ensured that we found a nice balance between work and play. He even invited all of us and our families up to his cottage every summer for a wonderful day of camaraderie, and everyone on the squad, and our families, ended up becoming good friends.

We were an extremely close-knit group, as we had to have each other's backs every night. Each team had a type of case assigned to them as their primary responsibility. Ours was prostitution, including street prostitution; escort and call-girl services, which were more difficult to investigate; and, by far the worst, going after those responsible for what would now be called human trafficking. Even back then, there was a steady stream of young girls who were being lured, or forced, into prostitution. They were often moved between Ottawa, Montreal and Toronto, and the men who preyed on them were extremely violent if the girls didn't do what they were told.

In one case, we were able to convince a girl to testify against two brothers from a well-known Nova Scotia crime family. The night before she was to testify, I got paged to call a phone number in Toronto. A friend of mine from Toronto Police told me that they had picked up the girl in a street sweep (where a group of undercover officers arrest a large number of street prostitutes). She told them that she had been kidnapped by our two accused brothers, driven to Toronto and put back on the street.

Frankly, I was amazed she hadn't been badly hurt, but I surmised that they wanted the money she could bring in from working the street. Remember, this was in late 1987 or early 1988. Human trafficking was, to most community members (and many police and justice leaders), not yet a real thing. At least not in Canada and especially not in quiet little Ottawa. Well, we knew different. So did she, and from a far more personal, and terrifying, perspective.

My friend stayed with her all night at the Toronto airport, bought her a plane ticket to Ottawa with his own money (getting approval for that kind of emergency expense would have taken too long) and put her on the first plane to Ottawa. I met her at the airport and drove her to court. She testified just hours after having been located in Toronto. Both accused got eight years in federal prison, which was almost unheard of then.

Sadly, and as we all know, the worldwide tragedy of human trafficking continues today. But at least Canada was spared from the involvement of those two guys for a while. While I felt proud of the young woman's courage and determination, I also felt bone-tired after the experiences of the past few days. However, I had no idea that being tired was about to become our way of life!

Chapter 8
Welcome to Parenthood

Nineteen eighty-eight was a fantastic year because Lise and I welcomed our first-born son into the world. We had just finished getting the nursery ready and had put the crib together only the day before. The labour was very long and difficult, about eighteen hours of pain for Lise while I did whatever I could to support her. She had decided not to get an epidural injection to help ease the pain, as she wanted it to be as natural a process as possible.

I will never forget the first few moments of joy I felt when I saw our son in the doctor's hands. The joy quickly turned into horror when I realized he wasn't breathing and had a dark-blue complexion. I could see that the umbilical cord was wrapped around his tiny neck multiple times, and the doctor and nurses had concerned looks on their faces. *Dear God. Please help our son. Please let him be OK!* Lise was oblivious to all this as she was lying back on the delivery table, crying. Both tears of joy and tears of pain, I'm sure. I did my best not to look frightened, but I was so scared that our little boy wasn't going to make it. Seconds seemed like hours.

In reality, the medical team was unbelievably quick to respond. The umbilical cord was clamped and cut then whipped away from his neck. A bit of suction and whatever else they did, and the blue was replaced with a rosy-pink skin tone as Jean-François Valcour came screaming into the world!

A couple of days later, having fought to keep Lise in the hospital to ensure that both she and Jean-François (who now goes by Jonny) were doing well, we carefully bundled him up and brought him to Lise's parents' home to show him off to the entire family. Lise was so protective that she wouldn't even let anyone open the car door. They all had to look through the window to see our bundle of joy.

Life was good.

•   •   •

Four months later, on the eighth day of the eighth month of 1988, apparently the luckiest day in the Chinese century, I got a phone call at home telling me to be in the chief's office later that morning. I was either in big shit or something very good was happening.

It was good; in fact, it was fantastic! Not only was I promoted to sergeant, but my partner was promoted to staff sergeant and our boss was promoted to inspector. While I would love to say that our advancement was related to all our hard work and dedication, the reality was that it was tied to just one investigation. It was a sensitive case that, frankly, our superintendent had messed up with the media. We were able to resolve the case fairly quickly and give him a reasonable "out" with the media. He had invited my partner and me to his house for a celebratory drink after the case was resolved, and there was no doubt that we were going to be formally rewarded in some way.

Promotions, always contentious, were different back then. The process was nowhere near as complex as it was by the end of my career. All we had to do in the 1980s was pass a knowledge exam from the Ontario Police College, then you were in the "pool" of qualified candidates and the chief could select anyone they wished, typically on the recommendation of his superintendents. In any event, our old boss left the squad to become one of the division's inspectors while my partner became the Enforcement Squad's new staff sergeant. I stayed on the squad, now as a sergeant, and was given a new partner.

After a few months in my new role, I had to complete my first quarterly assessment on my new partner who, as a detective, was technically working "for" me. Although our investigative teams didn't function like that day-to-day, and most decisions were typically made mutually, the fact is that policing was, and still is, paramilitary in nature and there is almost always a rank structure—meaning that when feedback has to be given or critical decisions have to be made, or if there is a disagreement about what to do, the sergeant is still "in charge." They are also the person who will be held accountable if mistakes are made.

I remember my partner reading the assessment at his desk and then a look of confusion came over his face. He finished reading and then turned to me saying, "Why is the first time I learn about something I'm doing wrong in an assessment instead of you telling me and letting me improve?"

Of course, he was 100 percent right. I failed in my job as a new supervisor in identifying the concern to him as soon as I observed it. By not doing that, I hadn't given him the chance to change his behaviour. I took the assessment back and changed it before submitting it to our boss. Lesson learned.

• • •

Our beautiful baby was doing well at home and, while the long hours at work and lack of sleep were adding stress to our lives, things were going pretty well. There were certainly times when we had arguments, and times when I found myself getting angry over little things, although nothing too over the top.

But our finances were beginning to cause me stress. When we were planning our family, we had jointly made the decision that Lise would stay home with the kids while I would continue trying to grow my career. Paying the bills on one salary was going to be difficult, but we had both agreed that this was the best way to go for us. Lise always did her best to help out financially, and she soon started a daycare service in our home. Having the extra kids around was a bit challenging, especially when I had worked late the previous day, but the additional money flowing in took some pressure off.

The bottom line is that, while things were good overall, some cracks were beginning to appear in our relationship. Nothing that normal couples didn't face, but the warning signs were there. I ignored them at our peril.

• • •

Early in 1990, we were blessed to welcome another beautiful son into our family when Dominic was born. Dominic's birth was much easier, so Lise said, and was certainly faster. The joy we felt with his arrival was ever so special, and his older brother was super happy to have a little brother to play with!

Things were becoming a bit tight in our little home, but we got by nicely. Lise suggested that we rent out the basement bedroom to help financially. I wasn't keen on the idea of other people living with us, but she was right. We could certainly use the extra money, even if it meant space would be even tighter. Over the next couple of years, we had some nice young women live downstairs, one from Toronto and two from Mexico. They were all in Ottawa to attend school and, in addition to helping financially, were a real help to Lise with our two children and the daycare as well.

While we tried our best to be good parents, the boys still had their share of mishaps. Jonny fell face-first onto a coffee table once and knocked out one of his front teeth. Fortunately, it was a baby tooth, so there were no long-term issues. Another time, we were visiting friends at a hunting and fishing camp near Renfrew. Jonny was quietly playing inside while we sat and had a drink a few feet away. Somehow, he found a metal clothes hanger that had fallen to the floor, and he proceeded to put the hook into his mouth. When he tried to pull it out, it went right through his cheek, making him look like a fish with the hook of the hanger poking out. That led to a fast trip back to Ottawa and a tetanus shot but, again, no long-term issues arose from the incident.

Not to be outdone, Dominic was motoring around our house in one of those "baby walker" chairs with wheels one day. Everyone had them for their kids back then, thinking it would keep them busy and help strengthen their tiny legs. We had forgotten to close the door to the basement, and down he went! Another trip to the Children's Hospital of Eastern Ontario, and he was diagnosed as being fine. The doctor urged us to get rid of the baby walker, which of course we did. It wasn't until 2004 that they were banned in Canada, but we had already learned our lesson.

While both kids continued to have the odd little mishap and get sick from time to time, they truly were wonderful children and brought nothing but joy to our lives.

• • •

I've never formally been diagnosed with attention deficit disorder, but I do not doubt that I suffer from some form of that condition. I've often heard people with ADD or ADHD talk about their minds being active constantly, like a mouse running on a spinning wheel in their head. For me, it's more like a globe spinning constantly, with a second axis rotating in a different direction, also in continuous motion. I can't stop my brain from bouncing from one idea to another, and it is extremely hard for me to focus on one thing at a time. No wonder my grade-school teachers were always telling me that I had "ants in my pants" and to sit down and focus.

Over the years, I learned techniques to try and manage my brain's constant barrage of inputs so that I could focus and get things done. Another thing that helped was always being challenged to learn new things. Subconsciously, this might be one of the reasons why a career in policing was appealing to me when I was growing up, because there are so many subdisciplines within the policing profession and so much variety in the job. And that certainly would prove to be true in my experience.

I again got transferred around 1990, this time to the Break and Enter (B&E) Squad. If you count my stint on Night Patrol as a formal "transfer" (it was really more like an internal assignment), this was my ninth move in thirteen years. I'm not sure if that was a record, but it certainly said something about me: no one wanted me on their team for very long! Another perspective, and certainly the one I took at the time, primarily because of my ever-growing ego, was that I was being groomed for further development and promotion. Having said that, I did struggle with each transfer, as I felt like I was just hitting my stride in a new role when I would get moved again.

Fortunately, my staff sergeant in the B&E Squad sensed my frustration and pulled me aside for a chat. He introduced me to Maslow's "hierarchy of needs" and explained that it was normal for people to feel the way I did after a transfer. Maslow's model puts our basic physiological needs—like air, food and water—at the base. These needs continue no matter what, until death. Moving up through the hierarchy, we encounter the higher needs of safety, love and belonging, esteem and self-actualization.

My boss explained to me that every time we are placed in a new situation, we can move down the model for a while. For example, when getting transferred to a new squad, we might not know everyone and therefore drop back to finding our place on the team and seeking a sense of belonging. Over time, as we get more experience and possibly take a course, it leads to our feeling much better about our ability to perform well and fit in. If we work at something long enough and become highly respected, we might achieve Maslow's top level of "self-actualization." This might, he said, be described as having reached your full potential in a given role.

Learning about these concepts really helped me as a relatively new non-commissioned officer, or NCO. Here I was, a sergeant on a new team where almost everyone on the squad knew more about investigating B&Es than I did, even though they were my juniors in rank. However, and this is a difficult thing for new supervisors to learn, my role wasn't just to use technical skills to investigate crime but also to supervise, manage and, hopefully one day, lead others. All three of these skills are very different from one another, and many people never get past the stages of supervision and management. Leadership is an entirely different thing—something I'll come back to later in the book.

Working in the Criminal Investigations Division also required us to work as partners. So, while each team of two normally consisted of a sergeant and detective (a constable assigned to CID for some time, who would revert to being a constable when transferred back to patrol), we worked more like a partnership than as a supervisor and subordinate.

I was blessed to have some great partners over the years, and working in the B&E Squad was no different. While most of my partners were great, I had one who was outstanding, not just for his abilities as an investigator but also for his insights into human behaviour.

• • •

"Put your book away," said my partner.

I looked at him like he had two heads. We were in the middle of taking a statement from an accused in a B&E case and sitting in an interview room in the cell block. Taking notes was my primary responsibility as the secondary officer in this case. My partner was the lead investigator, so he was doing the talking today.

Remember, this was long before there was audio or, much later, video recorders in the interview rooms. Anything, and I mean anything, that was not noted in our duty books was like it never happened. Not only did we try to get as much of what the interviewee (witness or accused) said, we also noted as much as possible about their behaviour and their demeanour. Did they seem nervous? Did they look right at the primary investigator when speaking, or were they unable, or unwilling, to keep eye contact?

And now, my partner, also a sergeant in this case, was telling me to put my book away and to not take any more notes. This had never happened to me before, and I had taken tons of statements over the past few years. But he was the "boss" on this case, so I did what he said. I closed my book, put my pen away and watched.

He seemed to get a bit smaller in his chair (the opposite of sitting higher to be in a position of authority), softening the tone of his voice to almost a whisper. He looked right into the suspect's eyes for a moment and said, "Listen, we have everything we need here for the case against you. You're going back to jail. There is no doubt about that. That's why I told my partner to stop taking notes. We don't need any more evidence against you." (All true.)

He went on. "However, there's something I'd like to know. Not as a cop, but as a human being. Why? Why did you do this? What's going on in your life that led you to this point? If you're willing, I want to help. Now, don't get me wrong. You are going to jail for what you did. I'm talking about when you get out. If you need help when you get out, I promise I will do my best to help you. I know lots of people and programs in the community that are there if you know where to look. But for me to help you, I need to understand why you're doing what you are doing. What's going on? Is it drugs? Alcohol? What's leading you down this path?"

I was listening to this and thinking, *Who cares? Why's he asking this guy these questions? We have everything we need to charge him and move on. What does it matter why he is doing the crimes?* I couldn't give a shit about this guy or why he did what he did.

Partway through my partner's one-way communication with the suspect, something happened that was unprecedented in my experience. The suspect's shoulders dipped and his head dropped. In the corner of one of his eyes, a small tear formed.

I get emotional even today thinking about it. My partner was talking to the man, not the suspect. He was connecting with him on a human level. A level of empathy that I had never witnessed before in my life. It was like they were connected and I wasn't even in the room.

I didn't move. I felt like my breathing even stopped. I was witnessing something very special. Two people, who minutes before were adversaries of a sort, were now on the verge of being truly open and connected with each other.

The man started to speak, saying, "It's the booze, man. I've tried to stop, but I can't. My life is so fucked up. I've lost everything, and I just don't know what else I can do."

My partner continued to talk to the suspect, not as friends but as someone who truly wanted to help a man who, at least at that very moment, desperately wanted help. At the end of the interview, my partner gave him his business card and told him as soon as he got out of jail to telephone him. He would help him find a program and would do whatever he could—as long as this man was committed to getting help and stayed out of trouble. If he broke the law again, my partner said, he would do his job and put him back in jail. But if he worked hard on his recovery, my partner would be there to help.

We all shook hands (something we just did not do with suspects) and left the cell block, with the suspect going back to his cell and us heading to the cafeteria for a coffee. I asked my partner, who had been the first officer in our police service to talk openly about being an alcoholic, to explain what had just happened. He had helped so many officers over the years by sharing his experience with addiction, and he now told me that, as someone who understood making mistakes in life, he was 100 percent committed to helping the accused when they got out of jail. He said he saw it as our job as police officers not only to investigate crimes but also to prevent them. And how better to prevent crime than to help criminals get the help they need to stop breaking the law—and possibly more importantly—get healthy for themselves and their families?

I have to admit that I was nowhere near empathetic enough at that stage of my life to truly comprehend what he was teaching me. Having said that, it certainly struck a chord in me and gave me something to think about.

Something that would later hit home in a very personal way.

•   •   •

A few months later, Lise and I were at a social event with my partner and his wife. At one point he looked at Lise and said something like, "How would you like to improve your marriage?" He quickly went on to say that he knew we had a good marriage, albeit still relatively new. His wife endorsed the idea while I was trying to figure out what kind of cult they were inviting us to join!

They told us about something called the Worldwide Marriage Encounter, or WWME, and that they had both been involved for several years. They said it was for good marriages that want to be great, not for marriages that were failing (apparently there was another kind of group for that). Lise was all for it, while I, in my typical "say no first" way, was extremely skeptical, to say the least. The more they spoke, though, the more it sounded like it might be a good idea. There had already been some cracks forming in our marriage, primarily around finances, so maybe this weekend away would be just what the doctor ordered.

WWME has various chapters depending on a couple's religion. We went to the Catholic weekend that was held at a church in Aylmer, Quebec. I was thinking we would likely have to listen to a few lectures, maybe participate in some group sessions and then have lots of time to spend by ourselves, napping, making love and just relaxing. That didn't sound too bad at all.

The reality hit me when the first session started and the presenting couple asked us to truly commit to the process and each other for the entire weekend. No phoning home or work. No watches. Full commitment to improving our relationship. I couldn't believe it, and I'm sure my body language was telegraphing my disapproval to the front of the room. However, when I looked at Lise, she was beaming. She was loving this and was "all in." Begrudgingly, I decided that for the sake of our marriage, I too would give it my best effort.

In the end, it was a fantastic weekend of renewal. Using the communication processes they taught us, Lise and I opened up to each other about several issues that were beginning to bother us. We learned some extremely useful tools, such as the "WIN" technique, to provide feedback to our spouse in a structured and constructive way: "When you _____, I feel _____. I need _____." For example, Lise might have said something like, "When you get angry and raise your voice at me, I feel sad. I need you to speak to me in a loving way, with kindness and respect."

We also learned the difference between feelings and judgements. They explained to us that saying, "I feel that . . .," is not really a feeling but a judgement. True feelings, on the other hand, are a "spontaneous inner reaction." So, my getting angry and raising my voice at Lise created a spontaneous inner reaction called sadness. I might loudly declare that I was upset over our finances (judgement), but the only way she could truly know how I was *feeling*, and the only way I would get through to her, was if I expressed it to her lovingly and respectfully. Perhaps something like, "Lise, when you spend money we don't have, I feel concerned. I need you to discuss major expenses with me before buying something that's not in our budget."

The workshop was very long and very tiring, both physically and emotionally, but by the end of it, our love for each other was stronger and deeper than it had ever been.

Before we left to go back home, my partner and his wife, who were one of the presenting couples that weekend, came to see us in our tiny little convent-like room. They looked at Lise and asked how she liked the experience. Lise was so happy and expressed her gratitude for their having believed in us enough to invite us to participate. I felt that—no, sorry, I judged—that something was coming that I was not going to like. I was right.

They then asked Lise what she thought about us becoming a presenting couple and said that only one couple per weekend might be asked to take the next step and learn how to present at a WWME retreat. While Lise was clearly extremely excited, I was not happy. Not happy at all.

With everything that was going on at the time, compounded by me working shifts, there was no way I had the time to put the necessary effort into presenting at one of these weekends. It was fine for Lise, I judged, as she had lots of time as a stay-at-home mother to work on preparing the talks. (See the judgements and air of superiority slipping in there?) I expressed my concerns to my partner and his wife, but they continued to focus on Lise. They had done this before and knew that the husband would be the one to throw up barriers and obstacles. Their way of dealing with that was to ignore me.

In the end, they succeeded in convincing me that this would be great for our marriage and that we would be able to help others experience WWME weekends the same way we had. Presenting couple we would be.

•   •   •

When I returned to work, I was very pleased when my staff sergeant told me that I had been selected to attend the two-week surveillance course at the Ontario Police College. In this highly sought-after training course, I would be learning the art of surveillance from some of the best in the world. (Unlike what you see on most police shows on television, surveillance truly is an art.)

As this was a course for experienced officers, we didn't have to deal with most of the bureaucracy and protectiveness faced by new recruits when they attended OPC. We were all in plain clothes, not suits or uniforms, and came from police services across the province and from a wide range of communities. A number of us who came from larger cities were placed on a team led by RCMP experts, but the principles and techniques they showed us were very similar to those being taught by other instructors, often from the OPP.

Each officer taking the course had driven a surveillance vehicle to OPC, as that would be our "classroom" for most of it. However, we also spent a great deal of time learning how to conduct surveillance on foot, which is more common in big cities and something that investigators working in smaller or rural communities would not have to deal with as frequently.

While I can't provide any details, for obvious reasons, about how real surveillance is conducted, I can say that it is an extremely fluid dance that requires clear, precise and concise communication. These skills need to be shared by a group of highly skilled team members who can stay calm, visualize spatially and work collaboratively.

No wonder this course was so highly sought-after. Although it was very demanding, it was also a huge amount of fun. And we were learning an important new skill set from instructors who had decades of experience, all while driving all over southwestern Ontario as we "followed" pretend bad guys (instructors who took great pride in "losing" us regularly). What's not to love about that?

•   •   •

One of the first lessons you learn as a new cop is to never walk past the boss unless necessary. Go out the back door or wait until you're sure they are gone for lunch or gone for the day. If you walk past the boss, there is a very real possibility that they are going to give you a job to do. A job that you probably don't want. A job on their task list that needs to be unloaded (aka delegated) on an unsuspecting cop, likely a rookie because veteran officers aren't stupid enough to be in the boss's sights during the day.

While I was on patrol, it might have gone down something like this: "Hey, Valcour, do me a favour [they are not asking] and give 14 Beat a scrub [another check before the end of shift]." Now that I was a sergeant in the B&E Squad, these kinds of unwanted tasks simply took on a different form, typically a new, hot investigation. Not hot because it was exciting or there was a hot lead; no, hot because someone—maybe the chief, after a call from an elected politician or another community member—called down to the investigative supervisor about it, wanting it dealt with right away. More like a hot potato.

Unfortunately, it was much harder to avoid the boss in a detective squad because, at least in Ottawa, our desks were right in front of the boss's office—an office that had a door but was glassed in so that they could see everyone on their team. So, when I heard my boss call out to me asking if he could see me for a minute, I felt like I was about to get screwed.

He told me there was some scientist at the National Research Council (NRC), part of the Government of Canada, who wanted to talk to a break-and-enter investigator. My boss had no idea what the guy wanted, but he needed someone to get right over there to talk to him. My boss knew I had a history of working on technology projects, so I was "the perfect guy for the job," he said with a smile (meaning it was now off his plate and onto mine). That might have been true. It was also very likely that I was the first investigator he saw after getting the call from the deputy chief. I was crazy busy with various investigations at the time (mind you, we were always busy) and, again, thought to myself that I was getting screwed because of my technology background. I had no idea at the time just how much this conversation was going to change my life.

I drove over to the NRC and was met by someone from a group called the Canadian Police Research Centre (CPRC), which was a partnership between the NRC, the Canadian Association of Chiefs of Police and the RCMP. I was told that this group was working with the scientist I'd been sent to meet with, on something called a "rules-based expert system." I had no idea what that meant but went with the CPRC rep to meet what could best be described as a "mad scientist." He was a diminutive man, likely around sixty years old, with a slight moustache and wispy hair that didn't seem to know where it wanted to land.

The scientist explained in relatively easy-to-understand terms that a rules-based expert system was a form of artificial intelligence. They were building on research that had already been conducted by Baltimore County Police in Maryland in the United States and Devon and Cornwall Police in the United Kingdom. They wanted to work with Ottawa Police experts, in this case, police investigators, forensic specialists, crime analysts and anyone else who might be able to help create "rules" for a computer system. The goal was to replicate how an investigator analyzes a B&E crime scene.

I thought this all sounded quite interesting but had no idea how it would work or what he wanted from me. When I asked the scientist exactly what he needed me for, he told me he needed a year's worth of data about all of our break and enters. Having worked on the CADRE technology project years previously, I knew that all of our computer data was stored in our mainframe computers on large tapes and would not be difficult to access, once we got the required approvals. After I had successfully delivered the data to the scientist's office, I continued with my life and didn't hear from him again for months.

•   •   •

Lise and I were still committed to being a presenting couple for Marriage Encounter, scheduled to take place early in 1992. Lise was pregnant at the time with our third child, due in April that year.

While we were both extremely tired, we worked on our talks together whenever we had a free moment.

These weekends in the Catholic church have three presenting couples: senior, mid and junior. Lise and I would be presenting the various topics assigned to a junior couple. The preparation process required that we start to "peel the onion" on our relationship and provide real examples, both of where each of us felt things had gone well and where they had gone badly. We had lots of great discussions and some fights but, in the end, we were both happy with our talks.

The weekend of our first presentation arrived, and off we went to the church in Aylmer. As the "junior" couple, we didn't have to present until Saturday morning. The Friday evening session was led by the senior couple, a loving husband and wife who had also led the weekend that Lise and I had taken the previous year.

It was fascinating sitting in the room and watching everyone arrive, knowing what we knew about how the weekend was designed and how it would unfold. As had been the case with us, most of the husbands arrived with their arms crossed and this look on their faces that said, "I'm only here because my wife is forcing me to be." Meanwhile, most of the wives looked happy and excited to be attending. Not to stereotype, but having given multiple WWME presentations, I can tell you that the women were more open to the experience, and it was 90 percent women who were driving this ship towards what they hoped would be a renewed loving relationship with their husbands.

Lise and I gave our first of three talks on Saturday morning. Much as I've done earlier in this book, we shared our upbringing, how we met, how Lise went off to backpack in Europe, how we met again, including the fact that I was engaged at the time, and how we eventually got married. We didn't hold anything back as we described the difficulties we faced, including how I was beginning to control Lise via my managing the finances and how I would sometimes drink too much, get angry and raise my voice at her, and treat her meanly. Lise explained that this made her feel small, disrespected and sad.

Lise cried. I cried. People in the room cried.

On Sunday morning, there was a long exercise that couples were to do in the privacy of their rooms, requiring them to truly open up with each other and share their innermost feelings, thoughts, desires and dreams. Like everything else in life, those who put the most into the weekend got the most out of it. Having said that, the vast majority of the couples who were there that weekend came back into the conference room after the Sunday morning exercise transformed, and we witnessed this at all of the WWME weekends we went to. No longer was the husband refusing to engage emotionally. There was a glow to most of the couples as they walked back into the room, holding hands and smiling. They radiated a renewed love for each other. It was amazing to watch.

A few hours later, we all said goodbye to each other and went our separate ways. Although couples were offered a chance to join a post-workshop group, one of which Lise and I led, this would be the last time we would see many of them. And for us, it was back home and back to reality. Back to me continuing to behave badly towards Lise, exactly as I had described in the wonderful, moving, transformational talks we had given the participants.

The problem was that I wasn't truly transformed myself. Deep down, if I had dared to peel the onion far enough to be fully honest with myself, with Lise, presenting at WWME was an exercise in continuing to build my ever-growing ego: *Look at me. Look what a great husband I am. Look how much I have changed. Listen to me and you, too, can be perfect!*

I'm not saying I was consciously thinking these things. No, I was unconsciously continuing the journey that had started years previously when, as a little boy, I did things to get noticed and be loved. By my mom. By my teachers in grade school. The helpful little boy who baked cakes with his mom instead of playing with his friends. The boy who offered to clean the blackboard and became the AV helper, setting up the movies for class and then staying late to put everything away.

I wish I could have understood the psychology of what was happening during our time in WWME and why I behaved the way I did. Maybe I could have done something to change course. Maybe a minor course correction back then would have made a major difference in our lives years later, just as a course correction of only 0.5 degrees by a plane leaving England equates to a massive change in where it lands in North America hours later.

My words to the Marriage Encounter group were deep, warm and designed to touch everyone's heart. But as the saying goes, "deeds speak." Secretly, at home with Lise, I was continuing to spiral downward. I was full of shit, and only Lise knew it. But she was too afraid to say it. Even to herself.

• • •

Mathieu Valcour was born early in 1992. The length of time from contractions starting to birth was, for us, a record. He was born with amazing blond hair and looked like an angel. We were so happy to have such a beautiful little family with three healthy, happy boys!

We soon realized that our small house in the south end of Ottawa wasn't big enough to raise our growing family. We found a much bigger home in Orleans with a massive backyard. By now, we had a great deal of stress in our lives, but this house was going to help solve all of that, and this was where we would live happily ever after with our three wonderful children.

Or so we thought.

• • •

"I can't do anything with your data, it sucks," was the essence of what the NRC scientist said to me when we met again months after I had given him the data tapes with all the break-and-enter files.

I told him I wasn't sure what he wanted me to do about it, as the data was what it was. I couldn't change it. He explained that we weren't gathering quality data at the various break-and-enter scenes and that we needed a new process to create "rules" that would allow the expert system to develop profiles of B&E suspects based on their actions at a crime scene. First, he said, a new form had to be developed to gather much more detailed information—enhanced data that could be leveraged by the expert system to develop general profiles. A specific profile would then be linked to an individual only once they were arrested and charged with their specific B&E. From there, each suspect's individual profile would allow us to identify them as potential suspects in future B&Es that had similar characteristics, or modus operandi (MO).

This made perfect sense to me as a seasoned B&E investigator. Break and enters are a "serial" crime. Most people, including most investigators, think of serial sexual assault and prolific homicide offenders as serial criminals. The reality is that break-and-enter suspects often, although not always, stick to whatever works for them.

Serial sexual assault offenders and murderers typically have an underlying fantasy or psychological gratification that drives their behaviour, classified (or profiled) by the Federal Bureau of Investigation (FBI) into types of offenders, such as "mission-oriented" and "power/control." In the case of break-and-enter suspects, a class of criminals who have had far less research conducted on them, their primary motivation is money—money to buy whatever is typically driving their addiction, be it booze, drugs, gambling or some combination of the three.

I won't bore you with the details of how we created the rules that drove the functionality of the expert system, and ultimately the new data-gathering form, but suffice it to say that many months later, we had everything we needed to move forward with the creation of this exciting new investigative tool!

• • •

One of the advantages of working on this project, in addition to having the time to focus on problem-solving, was that the CPRC, as part of the Government of Canada, could fund all sorts of research trips. Over the next couple of years, we had the opportunity to conduct research at a wide range of locations in both the United States and the United Kingdom.

For example, we met with profiling experts at the FBI's Behavioral Science Unit in Quantico, Virginia, visiting the same offices shown in the movie *Silence of the Lambs*. On the same trip, we met officials from the U.S. Department of the Treasury and the Jefferson Institute for Justice Studies, both in Washington DC. We also met with the research teams at the Baltimore County Police Department in Baltimore, Maryland, and the Devon and Cornwall Constabulary in Devon, England, both of which were extremely helpful and supportive.

These trips were all funded by the CPRC and provided us with a wealth of knowledge and information that allowed us to further our research immensely. They also helped to continue building my ego and inflate my sense of self-worth. *Look at me, a world traveller and hobnobbing with various international experts.* A legend.

In my mind, at least.

•   •   •

Remember that beautiful new home with a wonderfully large yard? When I was working long hours and travelling to all sorts of amazing new places doing research, Lise was left to manage everything on her own: three boys under five, the house, the flowers, the garden, the lawn—and all the weeds that seemed to spring up every night.

Things were tight financially with the new home and only minimal income coming from Lise's daycare business. She worked so hard at it and, as anyone who has ever run a daycare knows, it was very demanding. The parents, although well-intentioned, were often late picking up their children, adding even more strain to an already stressful environment. And the more the stress level rose, the worse I began to behave. I was working so hard for our little family, I deserved to have a few extra drinks the odd time. Or so I rationalized.

My anger and frustration over our tightly stretched finances were always just under the surface, and I was blowing up at Lise on an ever-more-frequent basis. "Why are you constantly complaining about money? I'm the one bringing in the lion's share of cash into this house!" I would say, my voice rising, often yelling. As if it were all her fault.

I was constantly thinking of ways to make sure that the bills got paid, even if they were a few months late. The pink "past due" letters (*Why pink?* I remember wondering) from various companies started to show up even more frequently. Being a problem solver, I figured out a way to pay one credit card off using another credit card, and then pay part of a bill with whatever room was left. Any downtime I had when not working for the Ottawa Police was spent thinking about how I could find a bit more money to pay another bill.

I consolidated our loans into even bigger loans which, in reality, just kicked the problem a bit further down the road. Eventually, we would be out of money again and I would blow up again. *Why can't you go back to work and make some "real" money? What are you doing all day, anyway? Isn't there a way you can bring in another child to babysit or another person to live with us?*

The reality was that Lise was doing everything she could, even starting a small business selling crafts at local craft shows. While she, too, had her moments of anger and frustration directed at me, it was almost always me who was behaving in an increasingly abusive fashion. She had no idea about the additional pressure I was feeling because I controlled everything to do with our finances. I never shared with her the things I was doing to keep us one step ahead of all our creditors. I refused to share this information in part because I believed, as it was how I had been raised, that it was the husband's role to look after his family financially.

I felt afraid, and that fear was beginning to manifest itself in the form of anger. Outwardly, it was anger at Lise for not helping out more financially. Inwardly, and unconsciously at that time, it was anger at myself. Once again, I was a failure. Once again, I couldn't do what everyone else could do. Once again, I was the stupid one. *Everyone else in my family is successful. Why can't I be the same?*

I couldn't understand how someone with my job, well-paying as it was, could get into this kind of financial difficulty. We should have had lots of money to pay the bills and look after ourselves, I felt at the time. Looking back, I believe part of the problem was that both Lise and I liked to live our lives for the now, to a certain degree. We took trips that we likely could not afford. We (mostly I) rationalized these decisions by saying that we didn't want to wait till we retired to live our lives. We wanted to have some fun now, not later.

My ego, and the need to be seen as successful, also played a role here. I wanted to be seen by the people I worked with and by our family and friends as intelligent, well-read, well-travelled. What other people thought of me was so critical that it made what Lise thought of me unimportant, or at least, less important. If she did or said anything that gave any kind of hint to others that we were having problems, I would fly off the handle later, in private. "For fuck's sake, why would you say something like that?" I would demand. "That's none of their business! What the fuck is wrong with you? Don't you understand how you're making me look?"

For the most part, my anger took the form of me raising my voice and taking control of the discussion. I had learned as a young police officer that the key to handling a situation is to take control immediately and establish authority. To use every trick at your disposal, from speaking in a loud and commanding voice, to "getting large" by standing tall and towering over others both physically and emotionally.

I saw myself as a world-class problem solver, and that only made matters worse. My job at work was to solve problems. It was not, at least early in my career, to listen to everyone's opinions and create a unified approach to potential solutions. No, my job was to understand quickly what the problem was, identify a solution and move on to the next problem. Despite what Marriage Encounter had taught us, and what I was saying when presenting at a Marriage Encounter weekend, I wasn't a good listener when I was in anger mode. I heard only the negative, the accusatory, the "You're not good enough" that Lise was, in my view, throwing at me.

While she might have been accusatory from time to time, in actuality, Lise was merely asking questions and trying to understand what was going on with her husband. Where was the kind, gentle man she had married? What happened to him? In my anger, though, I took her questions as accusations and veiled put-downs about my intelligence, my ability to look after my family and manage our finances and my worth as a person. More and more frequently I would go way beyond raising my voice, often to the point of actually screaming at her. There's no doubt the kids could hear this, but I didn't give a shit. In fact, our neighbours likely heard me yelling. *Fuck them.*

Anyone watching these interactions would have quickly concluded that I suffered from anger management issues and likely some form of passive-aggressive disorder. Not me, though; not then. All I thought was that I was being attacked. And, again, the best defence is a good offence—in my mind, at least.

I remember one time Lise accused me of being "abusive." Today people talk about trigger words. Well, that was certainly a trigger for me! I went off the rails, yelling that I had never abused her. "I've never touched you. I'm not fucking abusing you. I'm telling you the truth, you just don't want to hear it! I'm a cop. I know what abuse is, and this isn't abuse!"

To me at that time, the word abuse equated to domestic violence, which, by law, required a physical assault of some nature. As a cop, I knew the law. I believed that as long as I never hit Lise, then everything I was doing was justifiable. I adamantly refused to listen to any talk about me being abusive. I was a kind, loving, respectful husband and father.

Wasn't I?

Only a monster would be abusive to his family. I was not a monster.

Was I?

If only I could get Lise to understand that I was doing this all for her and the boys.

If only.

.   .   .

Everything at work was going smoothly in 1993. On the home front, at least from my perspective, things were a bit rocky but nothing to worry about.

Until I went for my annual physical checkup with our family doctor. All the tests were normal; however, there was one mole on my skin that the doctor was a bit concerned about. He sent me to a dermatologist to have it looked at. Although the dermatologist didn't think there was anything to worry about, he still froze the mole, cut it out right then and there, and sent it to be tested. A couple weeks later, I got the call saying that it was malignant melanoma.

I had cancer.

The specialist explained that there are three kinds of skin cancer, ranging from the least dangerous—basal cell carcinoma and squamous cell carcinoma—to the very dangerous melanoma, which was what I had. He also explained that there was no real cure for melanoma and the only way to treat it was to cut it out and hope that it hadn't already spread to other parts of the body, typically starting with the lymph nodes. If the cancer had spread to the lymph nodes, then it was game over (fortunately this never happened). He used much nicer terms and was far more empathetic than I'm describing here, but that was the message I was receiving.

On the positive side, he said, was the fact that they had found it early and that the mole was relatively "thin." The difference between one and two millimetres could change the prognosis from very good to very bad. He felt confident that he had cut all of the mole out, meaning that the risk of the cancer returning, at least at that location, was low.

I remember talking to Lise about all of this that night. I wouldn't say either of us was devastated, but we were both hit hard with the news. The fact that the prognosis was pretty good was certainly positive and helped to minimize our fears. We decided that we wouldn't tell anyone about my cancer diagnosis, primarily because I didn't want people at work looking at me differently or thinking that I couldn't handle the stress of the job on top of the stress of managing this new health challenge. As was the norm, I was looking at this from my perspective, not from Lise's. While it's true that I was the one with cancer, it was a family issue. My ability to see and understand that aspect of the situation, however, was pretty much non-existent.

So, I guess you could add "self-centred" to the ever-growing list of negative personality traits that Lise was facing and I was oblivious to. Many of the observations about myself that I am writing today were not even kernels in my consciousness back then. I wasn't *trying* to be a domineering asshole; I just was one. This is not an excuse, just my truth.

Overall, the cancer diagnosis caused us to reflect on life a great deal. Remember, starting from a very young age, I have always had a tremendous fear of dying. For most of my life to that point, I had done everything I could to not think about death, but here it now was staring me right in the eyes.

This health scare caused both of us to contemplate our lives and commit to living them more fully and with a deeper love for each other and our little family. The short-term impact was, in most respects, very positive for our relationship. But unfortunately, it didn't take too long for many of my negative behaviours to return. Certainly, my drinking, and the reasons why I drank, did not abate. If anything, I now had another reason, at least in my mind, to justify why I "deserved" to have a few drinks to help me relax after a long week.

•   •   •

Around the same time, I woke up one day with an extremely tender big toe on my left foot. It was swollen, felt warm to the touch and hurt like heck if I tried to move the toe—which you need to do to walk, of course.

I went to see our family doctor and told his receptionist the symptoms. She casually said, "Oh, you have gout." I asked what that was, and she called it the "rich man's disease." She explained that the men who get it (women have lower uric acid levels, so they don't get gout as often) normally drink a lot of red wine and eat large amounts of red meat. Well, both of these were certainly true for me, but I baulked at the idea that I, who was constantly struggling to pay the bills, could have something that "rich" people got!

Sure enough, after the test results came back, it was confirmed that I had gout. The doctor prescribed two kinds of medicine: one to help prevent a reoccurrence and one to help reduce the pain and inflammation when having an attack.

For those who have never experienced gout, it's hard to describe just how painful it is. I can tell you that I have had an infected wisdom tooth removed and I busted an eardrum while scuba diving in Mexico and then made the mistake of flying home the next day. Both were excruciating and right on par with the pain of a gout attack.

That first night after learning I had gout, I propped up my left foot on a pillow and loosely put the blankets over top in an attempt to fall asleep. It was our practice back then to sleep with the covers tucked into the end of the bed, and I hadn't had the foresight that night to pull them out to loosen the sheets even more. When Lise came to bed, she pulled on the blankets to bring them up to her neck as she usually did.

I screamed in pain as the blankets came straight down onto my big toe and Lise followed by screaming in fright as my screaming scared the heck out of her. A few minutes later, we could laugh about it, but at that moment there was nothing funny about the pain I was in. We learned a lesson that night that has remained all these years later: be sure to untuck the sheets from the end of the bed before going to sleep for the night!

Because it's a chronic disease, it was clear that gout would now be part of my life. There were certain things I could do to reduce the frequency of future attacks, primarily following an improved diet (fewer "purines" like red meat, certain seafoods and legumes like kidney beans) and reducing my stress levels. The dietary changes were relatively easy, but reducing my stress levels was something entirely different.

•　•　•

In 1994, the National Research Council researchers and I jointly wrote a paper, "The Investigator's Notebook,"[1] about the process we used to develop an expert system. They submitted it to the Proceedings of the British Computer Society Specialist Group on Expert Systems at Cambridge University in England, and it was reviewed, accepted and published by the Society. Subsequently, we were invited to speak at the British Computer Society Specialist Group Conference on Expert Systems, at St. John's College, part of Cambridge University, in England in 1994.

---

1. Brahan, J.W., Valcour, L. & Shevel, R., "The Investigator's Notebook." In: Milne R. & Montgomery A. (Eds.), *Applications and Innovations in Expert Systems II*, SGES Publications, Cambridge, 1994; 37–46.

Lise was ecstatic when I invited her to come to England with me for the event. Travelling together had always been a dream for the two of us, and this would be our first trip where we could combine business and pleasure. My brother and his wife were kind enough to look after our kids at their place in Oshawa, so we had that base covered.

We were first going to London for various meetings and then up to Cambridge for the conference. Because this trip was funded by the Government of Canada, I would receive a per diem to pay for my meals and incidental expenses. That meant we could eat well in one of the world's most expensive cities without going even further into debt. Lise was fantastic at finding places where we could eat inexpensively, typically by following working-class folks off the main streets and to the smaller more off-the-beaten-path spots that they frequented.

We took the overnight flight to London and got downtown fairly early in the morning. I had selected a small, but decent, hotel in the Mayfair area of London. Our room wasn't ready when we arrived, so we went "exploring." I knew where I wanted to go but didn't tell Lise as I wanted her to be surprised.

After walking through beautiful Green Park, we got to a spectacular building guarded by soldiers wearing their bearskin hats (something our youngest son would later wear for various ceremonies as a member of the Governor General's Foot Guards). Lise commented on how rich the person who lived here must be, and I smiled, saying yes, it was the Queen of England and this was Buckingham Palace!

While my colleagues and I were busy attending meetings with government officials at the Canadian High Commission or attending to additional work-related duties, Lise was out touring the city with the ninety-year-old father of a family friend. He was extremely spry for his age and, having lived in London his entire life and having been the driver of one of their famous black cabs, he was a wonderful and extremely knowledgeable host for her. I had only one day off in London and, with the help of our local friend, Lise had planned a jam-packed day of sightseeing for the two of us. We visited many main attractions, including London Bridge, St. Paul's Cathedral and a host of other fun and interesting sites.

We then took the train up to Cambridge and stayed near the university. Once again Lise explored the city while the rest of us attended, and eventually spoke at, the conference. We were all happy to win the "Best Presentation" award for our talk. Frankly speaking, though, I think the award was less about our speaking skills and more about the fact that ours was the only research that seemed to have any real-world, practical application. Most of the other sessions, were, from what little I could understand, all very conceptual and complex.

On the personal side, I found it pretty cool that a kid who had barely graduated high school was now lecturing such learned experts. While this was a great experience, it was also dangerous, as it continued to build my ever-growing ego and air of superiority.

•   •   •

Although 1994 was a great year in many respects, it was also the year that my cancer came back.

I went to see my dermatologist regularly, and on one of those visits he noticed a small growth on the edge of where he had previously cut out the malignant melanoma. Once again, he assured me that he didn't think that it was anything to be overly worried about. However, he froze and cut out another piece of skin just below my left breast. Sure enough, the results of the biopsy confirmed a reoccurrence of melanoma.

This time, surgery was the only option, and it had to be done at the hospital instead of in the dermatologist's office. The doctors took out a much larger portion of the impacted area in the hope of stopping any potential spread, and I was left with a large Zorro-like "Z" scar on my chest and was in a fair bit of pain for a few days.

I now had three doctors to see several times over the coming weeks: the dermatologist, the surgeon and an oncologist. The oncologist told me that he was putting me on some kind of experimental drug therapy that they felt was promising. Although it was not full-blown chemotherapy, the sickness I felt while on the treatment was certainly not fun.

No one at work knew anything about what was going on as, once again, I did not want anything to negatively impact my ability to move up in my career. I didn't want anyone to think I was weak. That was the priority in my mind. I told Lise (and myself) that my main concern was missing out on the additional salary, but, on reflection, it was likely much more about me looking good, strong, smart and successful.

•   •   •

Autumn was always a time of uncertainty in the police service. This was typically when the major transfer list came out and you would find out if your name was on it. Often you were told ahead of time by your bosses that you were going to be transferred, but sometimes not. I always wanted to think that the process was completely fair and designed both to help the organization and to further develop its members.

However, having been inside the room when transfers were being discussed with other senior officers later in my career, I now know that the process was, at least for managers, more about filling holes and slotting in recruits than it was about fairness or career development. Still, there are times when senior officers are trying to help individual officers who they believe have the potential for advancement (I certainly tried to do that as a senior officer when I became one).

In my case, I was approached by a deputy chief after a set of promotions was announced that I thought I had an outside chance of being included in. He told me that I had indeed been considered for a particular promotion. The problem they had was that no one could replace me in doing the research I was leading. Tough news for someone hell-bent on advancing, but he gave me some advice then that I took to heart and passed on to many other officers during the rest of my career: One of the first things you need to do when you get a new job or a promotion is start thinking about who is going to replace you. A part of your job is to develop a succession plan so that when the time comes for you to move on, for any reason, there is at least one, ideally many, who can replace you effectively and at a moment's notice.

I spent the next few months ensuring there was someone ready to take over the research. This effort paid off when my name was on the transfer list in October 1994. I was heading back to the platoon, my third stint there, this time as a patrol sergeant.

Many of my management and even leadership lessons came to me during this time as a patrol sergeant (more on management versus leadership later). One of them came from a senior constable, and it's a lesson that I would eventually have to relearn on my own, almost with very bad results.

One day I was managing a scene where a suspicious package had been spotted on Churchill Avenue in Ottawa's west end. Later found to be a functioning improvised explosive device, the package was discovered in front of a construction office, located at what used to be the Ottawa Police Force's west-end building. Because of the size of the device, our Explosives Disposal Unit (EDU) recommended that we keep onlookers quite far back.

You learn early in your policing career that it's easy to shrink a crime scene but almost impossible to expand it once it's set. Essentially that means that once all the crime scene tape goes up, like you see in the movies and on TV, people will stand right at the edge of the scene to try and ascertain what is going on. Having been "inside the tape" for most of my life, I never understood the fascination with police operations. It's gotten even worse over the years with everyone now having a mobile phone and filming everything in the hope of getting a scoop to share on social media or catching the cops doing something wrong. While we didn't have that pressure back when I was a patrol sergeant, we certainly wanted to get it right.

I ensured that the scene was large enough to allow the EDU guys to render the device safe, but I quickly realized that I didn't have enough officers there to manage the area adequately. To rectify the situation, I took one of the perimeter posts and stood there. A few minutes later, a constable with a great deal of experience, someone I knew well from having worked with him in the past, casually walked over to me and asked what I was doing. I told him we didn't have enough officers to fill all the spots, so I was taking one of them.

He gave me a quizzical look as if trying to figure out if I was being serious and then, realizing that I was, and that I was too inexperienced as a supervisor to see my mistake, he quietly, and very professionally, told me that it was not my job. He said that my job was to supervise the work, not to do the work. He recommended that I get on the radio and tell the dispatcher I needed more people here. They, and the staff sergeant back at the station, would figure out where to get the extra officers from. That was their job. We all need to do our specific job, not each other's.

I thought about what he was saying for a few seconds, thanked him for his advice, and then walked away as I spoke on the radio, telling dispatch that we needed more officers there to properly secure the scene. Lesson learned.

A few months later, I was the only patrol sergeant working in the entire city due to a couple of other sergeants having time off and one being tied up on something else. I was in the south end of Ottawa when a call came over the radio about an officer involved in a shooting in the far west end of the city. There was a car chase in progress, with the officers pursuing the suspect.

The chase was still active when I arrived in the area a few minutes later, so I did what most cops would do: I drove right past the left turn onto the street that would take me to the scene of the shooting and hammered the gas to try and catch up with the pursuit. I drove about eight hundred metres before I heard a voice in my head saying, *Not your job. Your job is back at the shooting scene.*

I came to my senses and turned around. There was valuable evidence at the scene of the shooting that would be instrumental in proving that our officer had followed all the rules, and critical for the detectives to determine exactly what had happened (we still investigated our own shootings back then). It was no longer my role to chase the bad guys. My responsibility was to stay emotionally detached and to ensure everyone else did their jobs properly.

This lesson resonated with me for the rest of my career. I was always thankful to that experienced constable for his quiet, and confidential, advice. This was something I tried to pass on for the rest of

my career, and even in retirement, to those who might need a nudge
in the right direction.

•   •   •

That Christmas, our little family went to New Brunswick to visit my
brother and his family of six children. We had a great holiday and,
of course, I got drunk a few times. To the best of my recollection, I
didn't do anything too stupid or obnoxious.

However, after being there for about a week, they decided to
watch *National Lampoon's Christmas Vacation* on the television. My
brother was laughing his ass off at the part where "Cousin Eddie,"
played by Randy Quaid, shows up with his family and their dog,
Snots, in a ramshackle RV. It was the first time I had seen the movie,
and I was sober enough to realize that there might be another reason
my brother thought the movie was funny.

Having now realized that we might have overstayed our welcome, I decided we should head back to Ottawa the next day. As the
famous Benjamin Franklin quote goes, "Guests, like fish, begin to
smell after three days."

Chapter 9
Pressure Cooker

Nineteen ninety-five was the year that things started to fall apart. At work, everything started well enough, with me continuing to work on patrol as a supervisor and Lise still running the daycare out of our Orleans home. But our tight finances, and my ongoing obsession with getting ahead at work in order to be seen as successful, added ever-growing stress to our lives. We were so stretched financially that both Lise and I lived in fear standing at the grocery checkout, not knowing if we had enough money in the bank to pay for the groceries we were hoping to purchase.

If you've never experienced that terrible feeling of helplessness, shame and embarrassment, then that's wonderful for you. Having to tell the clerk you don't have enough money for all the groceries, having to ask them to take away several of the more expensive items, like meat, and sensing the judgement from the other customers waiting directly behind you, has no equal in my mind.

All the stress we felt led to more and more fights—yelling, often screaming, matches between the two of us. Lise would get angry and, from time to time, yell or even swear at me. However, I was the one who continually went over the top, not hesitating to be mean, entirely disrespectful, and abusive in my language and behaviour. She was a caged soul, and I put her there.

That's how I see things today. Back then, I couldn't understand Lise.

I judged her as being unappreciative of everything I was doing for her and the boys. I concocted all these bizarre thoughts about her, like that she had married me just for my money and she was planning on leaving me and taking everything. She was the one, in my mind, who was manipulating the circumstances to her benefit. She was the one causing all the problems in our marriage. If only she could take the time to listen to me, to truly understand that everything I was doing was for our family.

Why can't she understand? Why's she being such a fucking bitch?

•   •   •

Nineteen ninety-five was also a tumultuous year of major change for the various police agencies in the National Capital Region of Ontario. After years of political debate and community discussion, the Ottawa, Gloucester and Nepean police forces amalgamated into one, and the Ottawa-Carleton Regional Police Service (OCRPS) was born. OCRPS would also, over the next few years, take over responsibility for various areas of the region that had previously been policed by the Ontario Provincial Police, including the small, but very rich, enclave of Rockcliffe Village.

I think it's safe to say that the vast majority of citizens who came from communities in the region other than the city of Ottawa thought this amalgamation was a terrible idea. Ottawa was, by far, the largest municipality involved, and other, smaller, towns were extremely fearful that their little police department, which they had controlled for decades, was far better and far more responsive than some massive new entity that was, in their minds, designed only to give additional tax dollars to the city of Ottawa.

I think it's also safe to say that the majority of the men and women who worked for the various agencies, including the Ottawa Police, had some level of apprehension about what this new service would mean to them and their families. The new police service covered an area of almost three thousand square kilometres, just smaller than the State of Rhode Island (3,144 km²). Would city cops get transferred from the police service they had joined to some small police station on the far end of the region, meaning lengthy trips and fighting traffic jams every day? What about where each member was in the "pecking order" of their service? Would this mean they would no longer get the transfer or promotion they believed they deserved?

On the positive side, at least from my perspective, we were now going to get rid of four separate dispatch centres, four different radio systems (that did not talk to each other) and two different records management systems (Gloucester, Nepean and OPP all used the same provincial system before amalgamation). These changes would lead to huge enhancements in information management and interoperability, the ability to share information between public safety agencies—a massive win for us as police service members and for the community we all served.

Practically speaking, at least at the beginning, the amalgamation only meant new uniforms and a new logo on the side of our cars. The rest would all be looked after by the bosses and politicians.

Despite all the changes swirling around me, my role as a platoon sergeant in the west end of Ottawa continued.

• • •

That same year, my binge drinking, infrequent as it was, was increasingly impacting our relationship. Once again, I would rationalize that

I deserve this, as I was working so hard to get ahead professionally. Although I didn't drink that often, when I did, there was still only one goal: get drunk. I would wake up the next day, often a Saturday or Sunday morning, feeling hungover, grumpy towards the kids and guilty about my inability to have "just one" drink. Why was it that others could have one or two drinks while I always had to get drunk?

The pattern of the last several years continued: I loved barbequing, as I could have a couple extra beers while outside, unnoticed. I would always make sure to buy extra booze for any event we were hosting at our place and would be sure to drink just a little bit faster than everyone else to get my "share" of the goodies. Once Lise and the kids had gone to bed, I would stay up "to watch TV," which was just my chance to sit and drink a couple large glasses of Grand Marnier. The kids would wake me up the next morning wanting to play, and I had no energy for them. I inevitably told them that Daddy was very tired, please play with Mommy.

There's a particular drinking-related incident that happened in 1995 (or close to it) that I need to share. I am extremely embarrassed and ashamed to share this story here, but I believe it's important for you, the reader, to see the level that I had fallen to as a result of my addiction to alcohol.

I had taken a trip with three Ottawa Police buddies to watch a Montreal Expos game. Before leaving Ottawa, one of the guys said he wasn't feeling well and volunteered to be the designated driver, which was great for the rest of us. We drank all night at the stadium and then went to a bar for more drinks after the game. Our designated driver then told us that he was too sick to drive, so I said I was fine and would drive us home. We had to get back that night because we were on the day shift the next day.

As I drove out of Montreal towards Ottawa, I knew that there was no way I should be driving. We arrested people all the time for doing exactly what I was doing. But I, like many drunks, thought that it would be OK, as I was "not that drunk."

It was pouring rain and visibility was terrible. As I drove, I was trying to stay in the right-hand lane and go the speed limit to avoid attracting any attention. A few moments later, I realized that I was now in the left lane. I thought, *OK, that lane is just as good as the right one, so I will stay here.* Suddenly, I was back into the right lane and then went off the right side of the highway. I jerked the wheel to the left but overcorrected. Our car flew across both lanes and went onto the opposite side of the highway. Knowing I was in trouble, I cranked the wheel hard to the right, causing the car to start spinning. We did one 360-degree spin on the wet highway and then another, at approximately 120 kilometres per hour. Everyone, fast asleep just seconds before, was yelling and trying to figure out what was happening.

After the second 360-degree spin, the car, miraculously, was now heading in the correct direction and I was back in the right-hand lane on our side of the highway. I pulled off at the next exit and told the guys that I couldn't drive any more. We fell asleep in the car for a few hours, and only then did I finish the drive back to Ottawa so we could get to work on time.

I allowed all of this to happen while I was a serving police officer, sworn to uphold the law. I'm not proud of what I did that night, and I'm still ashamed to admit those details now. Even at the time, I recognized that I had made a terrible error of judgement, and I vowed to go "on the wagon," to not let this happen again. I figured another benefit would be that I would have more energy for Lise and the kids.

•   •   •

To continue my career advancement, I decided that it was time for me to take some university courses. I knew that Lise and I didn't have the financial means to afford them, but I believed my professional development was a priority and went ahead anyway.

After researching a number of universities that offered distance-education courses, I enrolled in the Certificate in Public Administration program at Dalhousie University in Halifax, Nova Scotia. This was the same university my older brother, Gary, had graduated from with his Bachelor of Laws degree and it had (and still has) a great reputation.

I truly loved the experience and was grateful that the first course I had to enrol in was a class that taught adult learners how to write. It was outstanding. I learned more about various aspects of writing during those short months than I did in all of high school and, other than my typing course in Grade 9, it is the only class that taught me skills I have used almost every day of my adult life.

The problem was, as usual, that I needed to excel at these courses, not just get by. Whether it was my pride, my ego or my need to be seen as intelligent, I put everything into the courses, all to the detriment of Lise and the boys. When I was off work and at home, I was either reading, studying or writing. I had no time for them; school was my priority, second only to my policing duties.

The pressure just kept building. I had no idea that the dam would eventually burst.

•   •   •

That summer, Lise and I went to visit my old partner from the Break and Enter Squad (and from Marriage Encounter) and his wife at their cottage. He and I went fishing while Lise and his wife chatted at the cottage. As we fished, he told me a story about one of our civilian members who had saved up all his life to go on a nice trip with his wife after they retired. They had never travelled during his working years and focused on planning their once-in-a-lifetime retirement trip instead. Tragically, his wife passed away just months before he was set to retire, and they never got to take that special trip together.

That was a fear of mine and Lise's, putting travel off and never actually getting to do it. She and I always tried, even though we couldn't afford it, to live life for the present moment. With this in mind, we were planning our tenth-anniversary trip, a Caribbean cruise.

I asked my buddy while we were alone fishing if he and his wife might want to join us, and he gave me several reasons why they couldn't. Mostly, I surmised, he was afraid of getting seasick on the ship. I let it go for the moment but quietly planned to raise the question again later that evening.

At dinner, I looked at his wife and asked her what she would think about going on a cruise with us. I did to my partner exactly what he had done to me when he'd asked Lise what she would think about joining the Marriage Encounter presentation team. He didn't look at me or listen to any of my excuses that day, and I refused even to look at him while asking his wife to join us on the cruise.

I went on to tell them the story that he had told me that morning, about the couple who waited all their lives to take their special trip, only to have the wife die before they were able to go together. Admittedly, I laid it on pretty thick. However, I believed they would enjoy the cruise. My partner was a dessert lover, and I knew that if we could get him to the buffet table on a cruise ship, with all the ice carvings, foods from around the world and pastries galore, he would love it. Long story short, his wife loved the idea and the three of us were able to convince him that they should join Lise and me in October of 1995 for a cruise.

He was on the ship for less than thirty minutes when he came up to the rest of us, telling us all about the various desserts and how he was off to explore the ship (they subsequently took several cruises on their own). On the day of our tenth anniversary, Lise and I had a special dinner together. My partner and his wife had been kind enough to buy us a dozen roses while on shore in Jamaica, and we loved being able to celebrate with our dear friends.

At this stage, I had not had a drink in months. However, I thought it was such a special occasion that it would be a shame not to have a nice glass of our favourite wine, Châteauneuf-du-Pape. You might recall that my former partner had already revealed publicly that he was an alcoholic. He knew that I hadn't been drinking, but we never talked about it. I could sense he was a bit uncomfortable with my decision to have a drink at dinner, but he never said anything.

I've always loved red wine, and Châteauneuf-du-Pape in particular, but something weird happened when I took the first sip. It did not taste nearly as good as I remembered and I felt strange drinking it. It was almost like there was an unconscious part of me trying to warn me away. I drank half a glass of the wine and left the rest.

•   •   •

A month or so before we took the cruise, I was on a day off and at home when I got a call from work saying that I needed to be in the chief's office at ten o'clock that morning. I knew there was an outside chance of my getting promoted to staff sergeant but thought that I was likely a year or two away from that happening.

Sure enough, I got the promotion and was being transferred back to the Break and Enter Squad, now as the person in charge. I felt proud and was excited to tell Lise, our children and our entire family. My parents were extremely proud, and it certainly felt great to receive a number of phone calls, and even letters, congratulating me on this wonderful career advancement.

The first day of my new job did not start well. To save money, I had decided that I would start taking the bus to work. As a member of the police service, I got free bus transportation. This arrangement had been agreed to decades previously, the idea being that if there were off-duty cops on the buses, security would be improved. I don't know if that was true or not, but it certainly saved us money.

It was pouring rain that morning as I walked to the bus around five o'clock. I was leaving so early because I wanted to be the first person in the office. The bus stop was only about eight hundred metres from our house, but my boots were old and didn't keep the water out, so my feet were starting to get wet.

I was about four hundred metres from the stop when the bus arrived. Early. I had left in plenty of time, so I knew I was not late. Be that as it may, I started to run. I was sure the driver could see me, and I felt confident that he would wait.

He didn't. I missed the bus. On my first day as a staff sergeant.

I was livid. I swore out loud and felt cold, wet and hugely pissed off. Now I would have to wait fifteen minutes for the next bus and might not be first into the office. *Well, that just ruined my day. Fuck!*

I finally got to work just after six o'clock and was happy to see that I was indeed the first one there. I made the coffee, got settled in my office and looked forward to greeting everyone as they arrived. This first day on the new job wasn't going to be so bad after all.

I already had several ideas about ways our squad could improve based on the research I had completed for the expert system, which was all related to how various police agencies had worked to improve both their effectiveness and efficiency in B&E investigations. However, I knew it was important for the entire team to be involved in the process going forward.

One of the first lessons I learned in this new assignment, a tip that I've passed on to many over the years, is always to try to take over a team that is struggling. If at all possible, never replace an ace boss on an ace team. The previous boss of the B&E Squad was a great guy, but he was never given the resources to complete the job. Our overall statistics were terrible, and we had one of the worst B&E rates per 100,000 population in Canada. With only one plain car and one pager for six investigators, the team was understaffed and under-resourced. I was determined to find a way to improve the situation, and our performance, under my tenure.

A couple of days into the new job, I held a team meeting in one of the classrooms at headquarters. I highlighted our abysmal statistics and asked the others to identify the top one or two things that they thought we should do to improve. The first thing everyone wanted to talk about was the lack of resources. Several other complaints were voiced until I stopped them and walked to the whiteboard. I put a small dot on the board and asked the team if they knew what that was. I got some humorous answers but told them no, this was our "circle of influence."

I explained Covey's circle of influence as the things we could control: our attitudes, how hard we worked, teamwork and so on. I then drew a huge, if misshapen, circle around the tiny dot. I told them that this was our "circle of concern." These were the things we had zero control over, like the weather and the chief of police, among others. I told them that from this point forward we would be focusing entirely on our circle of influence. Things we could improve. So, I asked them, "What are they?"

One of the team's sergeants, a big burly guy who looked like a biker and who had a ton of experience as a drug investigator, spoke to the team. His extensive experience was matched by his keen intelligence, so when he talked about the need to identify the top B&E guys, follow them, catch them and put them behind bars, everyone agreed.

As it happened, the research I had previously reviewed was entirely congruent with this approach. I took his idea and many other suggestions from the other members of the team and drafted a memo to my boss. The memo included all sorts of data from various research papers in Canada, the United States and the United Kingdom. It recommended that we develop a new team to focus on what we called the "four-percenters," the small number of B&E offenders who commit the vast majority of offences.

I added some other recommendations, most coming from the team and a few from my research and experience. One was the need to stop investigating every break and enter. Research first developed in Rochester, New York, indicated that we needed to institute a policy of investigating only the cases that had a realistic chance of success and pointed to the use of "solvability factors" in determining which cases to follow up on and which ones would, at least initially, be immediately classified as "unsolved."

For example, attempted break and enters were never investigated. The traditional thinking was that if there was nothing taken, then there was no need to actively investigate and tie up limited resources. However, international research pointed to the fact that if there was a witness who observed the suspect, and maybe even scared them off, the chance of solving the case was greatly enhanced.

Whereas the majority of robberies (which require a human victim) are resolved successfully because of the nature of the crime, break and enters, for obvious reasons, have far fewer witnesses. In fact, the suspects, for the most part, work hard to be sure there is no one home at the time of the offence. They walk or drive around looking for obvious signs that the homeowner is away, all the ones we used to teach people who joined a Neighbourhood Watch, such as excessive mail in the mailbox and newspapers piled up at the front door (remember this was 1995; today it would likely be Amazon packages).

While a great deal of time and effort went into drafting the memorandum outlining our recommendations, we still had the practical problem of having only one car for all our investigators. One of the guys had the idea to put us all in the one car we had and have a photo taken. I took this photo to the bosses and told them that if they wanted us to be successful, we needed to target the four-percenters. And to target them required surveillance. Surveillance required vehicles, and we had only one, which is when I showed my boss the photo.

By the end of the month, we received approval to proceed with all of our recommendations, and the Break and Enter Response Team (BERT), now with five surveillance vehicles, was created. Thanks to some good luck and an outstanding informant, we were able to identify, follow and catch a group of commercial B&E suspects in the middle of a break-in during the first week of BERT operations! I came in the following morning to a room filled with tired, but smiling, investigators, seized evidence on a table being tagged and several accused waiting to be transported to court.

We had some more good fortune that first month, although I had to take quite a risk to turn a very negative incident into a positive opportunity.

I came into work on a Monday morning, still getting there first every day, and found a report waiting for me that outlined a horrific commercial break and enter at a major insurance company. This was not a typical break and enter where the criminals were in and out quickly, having taken the articles they valued. No, in this case, they were inside for an extensive period causing a massive amount of damage, including throwing their feces everywhere. It was, at least based on the reports I was reading, one of the worst commercial break and enters I had ever heard about in the city.

Later that day, after weighing the pros and cons and realizing I might get into some real trouble for what I intended to say, I decided to call the manager of the insurance company. I introduced myself and offered my sympathy that they were having to deal with such a terrible crime. I explained that, while their B&E was especially bad, we had thousands of victims every year and we were doing our best to improve our response times and solution rates.

I outlined our various new policies, the new BERT surveillance group and how we were still missing one thing that would truly help us do better going forward. I said, "I know this is going to sound terrible, and if my asking offends you, I understand. However, we have only one pager for all my investigators. I know this should come from the police budget, but there is no way I can get $500 at this stage of the fiscal year to rent them pagers." I had called the pager company in the morning to confirm how much it would cost to rent pagers for a year for all the investigators. "Would you be willing to donate $500 to our squad so that we can respond to informant tips even in the middle of the night and get out there to catch guys who are committing these crimes?"

There was a long pause, I'm sure because he could not believe I had the audacity to even consider asking a victim for money to help solve crimes. After several seconds, he replied, "Uh, yeah, that's likely something we could do."

A week later, everyone had pagers—and I had a new friend whom I came to know very well over the years. We still laugh about that phone call!

Another key component of our new strategy was to do everything we could to keep the four-percenters in custody. This effort was not focused on suspects (often kids) who committed one crime out of stupidity or drunkenness, on the contrary, we would work hard to get those kinds of one-off offenders back on track. No, we were scope-locked on serial criminal offenders who committed break and enters for a living. We put a full-court press on keeping them in custody and pushed local Crown attorneys to ensure they stayed that way.

Traditionally, Ottawa Police break-and-enter investigators would interview suspects to get information about other crimes or maybe to try and get a gun off the street. We would make deals with them, saying, "We will tell the Crown that you helped us out and ask them to release you right away." In large part, we created our own problem by using that tactic. Sure, suspects who co-operated helped us solve more break and enters and increase the team's resolution rate, typically by around 20 percent; but in the process, we were releasing back out onto the street the very people who were responsible for the largest number of B&Es, allowing serial offenders to continue being four-percenters and in the long run committing even more break and enters than we could resolve. Instead, our top priority needed to be the prevention of crime not the successful "resolution" of it.

This issue had bothered me for years and, again, my research supported my position. I would regularly ask my bosses, "Which would you prefer, that we prevent someone from breaking into your home and stealing items that have a great deal of sentimental value to you, or that we resolve it quickly?" Of course, 100 percent said that they would prefer we prevent the break-in.

Resolving this issue of releasing serial offenders early was also the subject of one of the recommendations in my memorandum. As a result, we changed our policy and, where legally appropriate, began focusing on putting the four-percenters in jail and keeping them there, rather than cutting deals with them and letting them go. We knew our resolution rate would go down, something traditionally considered a bad thing, but we were confident that the total number of B&Es would be reduced by the end of the year. If that prediction proved accurate, we would consider ourselves successful.

Well, drop they did. The 1996 *Juristat* report from Statistics Canada showed that Ottawa had the greatest decrease in break and enters in the country. The country! According to the report, "Vancouver reported the highest rate by a wide margin among the nine largest census metropolitan areas (CMAs). Rates fell in five of the nine CMAs in 1996, with Ottawa reporting the largest decrease (−16%)."[2]

Later, the report went on to break down the numbers in more detail:

> *Only Ottawa (−9%), Edmonton (−6%) and Toronto (−2%) showed decreases in the rate of residential B&E in 1996 (Table 5). Ottawa's decrease follows three years of growth, including a 31% jump in 1995. Police in Québec City (+21%) reported the greatest increase in 1996.*
>
> *Business B&E fell in five of the nine CMAs, with the largest decrease reported in Ottawa (−29%). Of the four cities showing increases, Québec reported the greatest growth in 1996 (+17%).*[3]

When researching the report, the author had called me seeking to understand why our numbers had improved so quickly, and he had given a nice shout-out to our work, and the B&E Expert System, in his findings:

> *The Ottawa-Carleton Regional Police Service is an example of a police department attributing their recent decline in B&E to special initiatives. Recently, their B&E unit established special surveillance teams and began using innovative investigative software to compile detailed information on each B&E. These detailed data allow the police to profile likely suspects, and the surveillance teams*

---

2. Rebecca Kong, *Juristat*, Canadian Centre for Justice Statistics, Breaking and Entering in Canada, 1996, Statistics Canada – Catalogue no. 85-002-XPE Vol. 18 no. 5, 1.

3. Ibid, 4

are assigned specifically to catch the suspects. The unit's strategy is
simple: if they are able to keep those few offenders responsible for
the majority of B&Es off the streets, the incidents of B&E should
decrease.[4]

After the *Juristat* report was published, we received phone calls from all over Canada asking what we had done to achieve such a reduction in our crime rate. Once we explained, other police services started implementing new policies, solvability factors and their versions of BERT, including the Ontario Provincial Police. Our circle of influence had grown from a tiny dot to a nice big ring. Still much smaller than our circle of concern, but even that had shrunk while our circle of influence was continuing to expand.

But I get ahead of myself here.

•   •   •

Looking back, 1996 was the year that would change our lives forever.

Almost my entire attention at the beginning of the year was on work. Things were going extremely well, and the team was firing on all cylinders. Any free time I had was spent focusing on my distance-education classes at Dalhousie University—where I was also rocking it with outstanding marks.

I was so preoccupied with those two things that I failed to comprehend, or possibly was too afraid to consider, what was happening at home. The stress of our terrible finances, my desire to get great marks in school and my obsessive need to be seen as successful at work were all building to a boiling point. When I did take the time to talk to Lise, I was constantly short and disrespectful, often boiling

---

4. Ibid, 5

over and becoming emotionally and verbally abusive. "What's wrong with you?" I would yell. "Don't you fucking trust me? I'm doing everything I can to make everything work. I don't need your bullshit right now."

I couldn't understand what her issue was. *I was working my ass off, being successful for her and the boys and wasn't even drinking. My last drink had been the half-glass of red wine on our anniversary cruise the previous October. What the hell else did she want from me?*

Unknown to me, Lise felt like a caged spirit, so desperate for help that she had reached out to my old partner's wife, who was providing her with advice and support. One of the things she recommended was that Lise start attending Al-Anon,[5] a support group for people who are worried about someone with a drinking problem. Lise did not see this as an alcohol problem, but an anger management issue. However, she was willing to take help from anyone who could provide it and was thankful for the lessons she was beginning to learn at Al-Anon. One of Lise's key takeaways from these sessions was that she had to stop "enabling" me and set boundaries. This was not easy for her but, after a time, she committed to doing just that.

On Sunday, January 28, 1996, I found out exactly what that meant.

---

5. al-anon.org

Chapter 10
Please Leave!

Please leave!" These were the words that Lise uttered to me, whispered really, at the end of yet another argument-filled Sunday. Words that would change our lives forever.

I have no idea what the argument was about, only that, once again, I had gotten extremely angry and taken it out on her. This time was different, though. She was no longer trying to match anger for anger; she was taking a different approach, and it was confusing the hell out of me. It didn't follow our typical pattern: friction point followed by me getting angry, followed by her responding in a similar but nowhere near as disrespectful manner, followed by the two of us separating and cooling down for a few hours (or days sometimes for me), followed by making up.

This time, though, she was not getting louder, she was getting quieter, softer and somehow more resigned. She started crying, saying that she couldn't take it anymore. She said that if I truly loved her, I would go away, maybe stay in her parents' basement. She begged me to get help because what I had become was not who I was. She told me that she thought I was sick and needed to get professional help.

At first, I just got angry, thinking that my strategy of the best defence being a good offence had always worked before. Not this time, though. Somehow, she seemed calm. Committed. Resolute. Once that became clear to me, I decided that I needed a new strategy. *Yelling isn't going to work this time.* I truly was thinking in those terms. I was not empathizing with the woman I loved. I was not allowing any of her sadness, hurt or pain to get anywhere near my heart, my soul. I was merely looking for a solution to this new problem. *I have to find a way out of this. I have to get Lise to stop talking about me leaving. I just need to get her off my back one more time and things will be OK.*

There's a saying I've learned over the years since that day: How can you tell if an alcoholic is lying? When their lips move! That was me. I would have said anything to get Lise to back down at that moment.

How will I look if we get separated, or even worse, divorced? What will my parents think? What will people at work think? Here we go again. A fucking failure. All of this was flashing through my mind during this exchange. Not love for Lise or my boys. Not a sense of caring and compassion. Nope. Only, *How will I look?*

I begged Lise to give me a week to figure things out and to get some help for anger management. The truth was that I was just looking for time to find a way to get her off my back and to change her mind about this ridiculous idea of me leaving the family home. *If I can get her to back down now, she'll forget about it and things will go back to normal.*

Reluctantly, Lise agreed to give me a week. She set ground rules and told me that if I got angry again and yelled at either her or the boys, then the deal was off. If she asked me to leave again, then I had to promise her right then that I would do it. I would go to her parents' or a friend's house (we had no money for a hotel room) or the YMCA or wherever. She was in control now, or so I let her believe. Or so I thought I was letting her believe.

I did not yet understand that the old Lise, the one that I could manipulate, control and dominate, was gone. Forever. The new Lise was here, like a fresh flower that's just beginning to bloom, or bloom again. Or at least she was beginning her own journey.

The following day at work, I did two things. First, I called my academic advisor at Dalhousie University and told him that I needed to stop taking courses for now. I said that I was having some difficulty at home and needed to spend more time there. He was supportive, telling me that I could always come back and continue later. For now, he said, focus on getting things better at home.

The second thing I did was call the Ottawa Police Employee Assistance Program (EAP) and ask to speak to someone about what was going on. Frankly, I thought the EAP was for losers who didn't know how to manage their lives properly. I had been raised to pray to God and to work harder. Those two things were all I needed to solve any problem, I believed. But I didn't have a problem. Lise had a problem. I just needed help in figuring out how to get her to realize it.

●   ●   ●

On Thursday, February 1, 1996, I walked down Elgin Street at the end of the day to meet Dr. Joe Dietrich. He was the psychologist that the EAP program had arranged for me to talk to. The session started off well. He seemed welcoming and open to anything I wanted to tell him. I proceeded to spend the next fifty minutes ranting about all the ways that Lise didn't appreciate me. That she was the problem and that if she would just try to understand how hard I was working to make our lives better, we would all be better off.

He asked me several questions, including about my alcohol use. I explained that I used to get drunk from time to time but had had only a half-glass of wine in the past year or so. At the end of the session, he said, "OK, I will see you back here, same day and time next week. In the meantime, I want you to go to Alcoholics Anonymous because you are a dry drunk."

I looked at him like he had two heads, but I didn't say anything. I still didn't trust the EAP program not to rat me out to the police service, so the last thing I was going to do was antagonize the doctor who was "treating" me.

I walked to the bus stop in a daze, thinking, *What the fuck is wrong with this guy? Didn't he listen to a word I said? This isn't about me, it's about Lise. She's the problem here, not me. Why couldn't he understand that? What a fucking asshole! And what the fuck is a dry drunk? I might have a few issues with anger management, but that's got nothing to do with booze. For God's sake, I've had a couple of sips of wine in the past year. What the hell is wrong with this guy?*

On the bus home, I kept repeating those thoughts over and over while also thinking about what I was going to say to Lise because she knew I was going to see the EAP doctor that day. After getting off the bus, I started walking home but decided to take a detour to go see my old partner who lived right around the corner. As I said earlier, he had openly admitted to everyone at work that he was an alcoholic. He had since done special training in addiction and had even given lectures to the different platoons about it on training days. He would know what the hell a dry drunk was.

I knocked on his door and, after he opened it and greeted me, I don't think I even said hello. Instead, I jumped right in and immediately asked, "What's a dry drunk?"

He gave me a knowing smile, chuckled in the way only he can and said, "Come on in, I've got a pot of coffee going, let's talk."

I told him what the doctor, whom he knew, had said about me

being a dry drunk. My buddy then explained that in Alcoholics Anonymous,[6] or AA as they called it, a dry drunk was someone who was no longer drinking but who continued to display the same kinds of behaviours and hold the same attitudes and beliefs as when they had still been drinking.

He continued speaking, but I was now lost in my mind. I was trying to figure out what this meant for me and how I was going to solve it nice and quickly. *I don't have a problem with alcohol, so how am I going to deal with this new hurdle?* I needed to continue doing whatever it was that I needed to do to keep being successful in life.

At the end of our chat, he told me that he was going to an AA meeting that night, right there in Orleans. Did I want to come along, he asked. I politely declined, saying that I didn't think that alcohol was the problem. He told me when and where the meeting would be held, just in case I changed my mind.

I walked home, where Lise was waiting for me. I told her what the doctor had said about me being a dry drunk and about my conversation with my ex-partner. I didn't tell her what I had told the doctor about her being the problem, as I figured that wasn't a good strategy when trying to get back in her good books.

She seemed to agree with me that alcohol was not the issue; she still believed it was anger management. She was disappointed that the doctor hadn't talked about that. At the same time, she seemed somewhat satisfied that I was at least trying to get some help.

Over the next couple of hours, I kept thinking about the AA meeting that was about to happen a short distance away. I had a vigorous internal dialogue going on about the pros and cons of attending it. *If I go, it'll show Lise that I'm serious about getting help. That'll get her off*

---

6. www.aa.org/

my back, right? But what if someone I know sees me? Fuck, I can't be seen in a room with a bunch of fucking drunks.

In the end, I decided to go, mostly just to make it look like I was willing to try something, anything, to get the relationship back on track. I put on a baseball cap and wore sunglasses so that no one could recognize me, but I went. When I walked through the door, I looked around and could not believe what I saw. The room was filled with absolute losers. These men and women had no idea how to be successful like I was. *They're a bunch of fucking drunks. What the fuck am I doing here with them?* The meeting proceeded, with me only partially listening, certainly not truly hearing anything they were all attempting to share. I just couldn't wait to get out of the door and back home.

My buddy came up to me after the meeting and asked what I thought. I lied to him, saying that it was OK. He handed me a pamphlet, "The 20 Questions of Alcoholics Anonymous," and suggested that I take it home and fill it in. I glanced at it and said OK, and asked for a second one so that I could get Lise to fill it in as well. *Why not get her opinion*, I thought. *It will show her I'm serious here!*

When I got home, I told her about the meeting and that I didn't think it was for me. However, I said, "Let's do an exercise where we both fill in this twenty-question survey. I'll fill it in for myself, and you fill it in thinking about my drinking. We'll do it as individuals and then compare what we said when we're both done." She agreed and walked away to complete the questionnaire, and I sat down with a pen.

I started filling it in and was happy to see the first question was "Do you lose time from work due to drinking?" I smiled as I filled in the "No" box with a big bold X. *So far, so good!* However, a few minutes later, I looked down and saw that I had fifteen "Yes" and only five "No" answers. It was then that I noticed the small print at the bottom of the form:

If you have answered YES to any of the questions, there is a definite warning that you may be an alcoholic. If you have answered YES to any 2, the chances are that you are an alcoholic. If you have answered YES to 3 or more, you are definitely an alcoholic.

I was gobsmacked! I couldn't believe what I was reading. *Am I an alcoholic? What the fuck is going on here?*

Lise came back into the room and sat down with me. I told her that I gave myself fifteen yes answers. She looked down at hers and said she gave me only twelve. *Only twelve. Fuck.*

We talked into the night and, somehow, I felt like something had changed. It was like something had gone *Click* in my mind and a new door had opened. I didn't know what it meant or if I was actually an alcoholic, but something had certainly happened in my brain. In my heart.

The next day at work was a daze as I tried to process what all of this meant for me. I had no idea. That night, Friday, February 2, 1996, I went to my second AA meeting. Once again, my buddy told me that he was going and where it was. It was called the Alta Vista Open Door and took place in a church basement on Alta Vista Drive, in Ottawa's south end.

This time I didn't wear a baseball cap or sunglasses. I parked my car in the large lot and walked towards the door. A few people were standing outside, smoking and chatting. They all smiled at me and said hello. I said hello, opened the door and walked downstairs. At the bottom of the stairs, a lady smiled at me and said, "Hi, my name is Jo, thanks for coming."

I looked around the room and was amazed at how different it was from the night before. This room wasn't filled with losers like the previous night. It seemed to be filled with people who were kind, who cared about me and who were all there doing the same thing I was, trying to get healthy. I was amazed at how different these people seemed compared to just twenty-four hours earlier.

This time I heard all the words during the meeting. There were two people, including my buddy, at the front of the room leading the evening. They opened by introducing themselves and then invited anyone who wanted to join them in reciting the Serenity Prayer:

> *God grant me the serenity*
> *to accept the things I cannot change;*
> *courage to change the things I can;*
> *and the wisdom to know the difference.*

I had heard this well-known prayer before, but never said by several people at the same time, and certainly never with what appeared to be true conviction.

Over the next hour, various volunteers went up to the front of the room to read things like the Twelve Steps and the Twelve Promises. Someone read a few AA slogans, things like "One day at a time" and "Let go and let God" and then explained what the slogans meant to them. They invited that night's speaker, a member of the group, to come to the front and he told his story. He talked about his life growing up, what happened with alcohol, how he got involved with AA and what it was like now. He was a normal guy with a story not overly similar to mine, but there were certainly some parallels.

Finally, and I'll never forget this, the door greeter, Jo, was invited up to hand out the "chips." She explained that the AA program in Ottawa had a chip system. You got a different coloured poker chip at various stages of sobriety. As I listened to her speaking, I was in a daze. I wondered how a kind, loving, respectful young man, whose marriage was wonderful for so many years, had messed up so badly. *What the hell happened?* I thought. *How'd I fuck things up so badly?*

I heard Jo say, "And now for the most difficult chip. It's called the desire chip. It's white and is here for anyone whose life has become unmanageable. Is there anyone who would like to come up and get a white chip?" Someone stood up and started walking to the front. The room erupted into applause, and you could genuinely feel a surge of happiness and positive energy flow through the room. A second, third and fourth person stood and walked up to get their desire chip. The room went crazy. I later found out that this was a record number of people to get the white chip at any meeting in the history of the Open Door!

As I sat there witnessing this, I thought about Lise, the boys and my family. I felt so emotional, so deeply sad. I started crying. *I love them so much, so very much. Things can't keep going the way they have. I'm going to lose everything if I keep going the way I'm going. I fucking can't keep going like this. I'm so fucking tired of hiding everything from Lise, from everyone. Fuck it. I have no fucking idea if this AA shit will work, but I can't keep going the way I have been.*

My life truly had, as Jo said, become unmanageable. I didn't know if I was an alcoholic, but I did know that I wanted things to change. I couldn't take the constant pressure of always having to look so good, so smart, so successful. I couldn't take what I had become. What I had done to Lise and the boys

At that stage of my policing career, I'd been involved in some pretty scary situations, a number of them literally life or death—car chases or pointing my firearm at a suspect, a fraction of a second away from pulling the trigger. Despite that, I'd never felt so scared in my life as I did in that moment.

I stood up, the fifth person to do so, walked to the front of the room, took a chip from Jo, who also gave me a wonderful hug, turned with my head down looking at the floor and walked back to my chair to a room filled with applause. In a room filled with love, acceptance and empathy. Although the long journey was just beginning, I had taken my first step in AA.

My life was unmanageable, and I wanted it to change.

•   •   •

I went for a coffee after the meeting with my friend and we talked for quite a while. I had a ton of questions, and he was both understanding and forthcoming, sharing the wisdom he had gained from years of attending meetings like the one we had just left.

I drove home and told Lise all about the meeting. I showed her the white chip and explained what it meant. She seemed both hopeful and wary at the same time. Looking back, I'm sure she was wondering if this was just more bullshit designed to get her off my back for another short period of time. I did my best to explain to her how different I now felt, but we both recognized that attending one or two AA meetings and getting a white plastic poker chip was not magically going to solve all my problems or bring trust and respect back into our marriage. We were both realistic enough to know that I needed to continue getting professional help on top of attending meetings regularly.

The good news was that we were now both committed to doing whatever it took to keep our marriage alive and, hopefully, someday, after a great deal of work, make it grow and flourish.

Chapter 11
One Day at a Time

You might recall the story of me missing the bus to work and my strong negative reaction. Well, the same thing happened on the Monday morning following my accepting the white chip at the Open Door AA meeting. I thought I was on time but, sure enough, the bus was early again and I was going to miss it. This time, though, I stopped and said the Serenity Prayer with an emphasis on "to accept the things I cannot change" (like missing a bus). I took a deep breath and said to myself that I would get the next one and everything would be OK.

I know this sounds a bit simplistic for the majority of readers, possibly even slightly crazy. However, for those of us who are wired differently, where little things become big things very quickly and trigger negative thoughts and behaviours, this prayer was already making a major difference in my life. Over time I came to realize that I couldn't change anyone else, not even Lise. The only person I could change was myself, and only if I worked hard at it and got help.

Lots of help.

• • •

While things were beginning to change for the better at home, I still needed to focus on my work and continue to lead the Break and

Enter Squad. Lise and I agreed that, other than telling close family members, the fact that I was now accepting that I was an alcoholic and attending AA meetings needed to stay a secret. We agreed that I needed to find more work–family balance in my life, but my policing career was, at least for now, our primary source of income and we couldn't do anything to negatively impact that employment.

That's not to say that I would have been fired for admitting I was an alcoholic. Not at all. However, back then, there was a strong stigma attached to addiction (and unfortunately, there still is today). That stigma had a way of splashing over onto potential career opportunities, and we both agreed that limiting my chances for further advancement would not be in our family's best interests.

There's no doubt that the new life I was just beginning to live— what I consider to be the second half of my life—was led by a much more empathetic, understanding and caring person. However, it's not like a switch was flipped and, all of a sudden, I became a wonderful guy, full of love and compassion. No, it was a very long, very hard and very tumultuous journey, especially for Lise. She had been hurt so much and so often by me that it would take years, and her own healing journey with professionals, for things to improve. For her to begin to trust in me again. For our relationship to grow.

But we were nowhere near that yet. In autumn of 1996, we were still far closer to ending our marriage than celebrating it.

•   •   •

Over the following months, I continued to attend AA meetings and started to work through their Twelve Steps, widely known about but few outside of AA know exactly what they say. They are reproduced here in their entirety.[7]

———

7. www.aa.org/assets/en_US/smf-121_en.pdf

The Twelve Steps of Alcoholics Anonymous

1. We admitted we were powerless over alcohol—that our lives had become unmanageable.

2. Came to believe that a Power greater than ourselves could restore us to sanity.

3. Made a decision to turn our will and our lives over to the care of God *as we understood Him.*

4. Made a searching and fearless moral inventory of ourselves.

5. Admitted to God, to ourselves, and to another human being the exact nature of our wrongs.

6. Were entirely ready to have God remove all these defects of character.

7. Humbly asked Him to remove our shortcomings.

8. Made a list of all persons we had harmed, and became willing to make amends to them all.

9. Made direct amends to such people wherever possible, except when to do so would injure them or others.

10. Continued to take personal inventory and when we were wrong promptly admitted it.

11. Sought through prayer and meditation to improve our conscious contact with God, *as we understood Him,* praying only for knowledge of His will for us and the power to carry that out.

12. Having had a spiritual awakening as the result of these Steps, we tried to carry this message to alcoholics, and to practice these principles in all our affairs.

A tricky issue for many people is the concept of a higher power and the many references in the Twelve Steps to God. There's no doubt that the founders of Alcoholics Anonymous were Christians and religious men. Bill W. and Dr. Bob (we never use our last names in AA to protect each other's anonymity) founded AA in 1935 in Akron, Ohio. While it has come a long way since then, the basic tenets of the program have, I'm told, remained fundamentally the same for close to one hundred years.

One of these principles is the belief in a higher power. For many, this is God, but for others who have suffered a great deal and who have lost their faith, or were not raised to believe in God, this is a bridge too far. Instead of allowing them to get stuck on that concept, AA teaches alcoholics that they can believe in whatever higher power they wish. For some, it is nature or the universe, and for others it might be some other form of deity. This is why the second step says, "Came to believe that a Power greater than ourselves could restore us to sanity."

Although Bill W. and Dr. Bob likely both meant God, there is no requirement for anyone to believe in a god to reap the benefits of AA. No one is ever asked to declare who or what their higher power is. This is deeply personal and everyone in the program is free to believe, to not believe or to even skip Step Two. For me, my higher power is God; however, as I was to learn a bit later in my recovery, exactly what God I believed in was going to change. More about this later.

My AA sponsor, my old B&E Squad partner, was instrumental in my growth in so many ways. In the beginning, he was simply available to me so I could ask him questions, or to give me tips and advice. One piece of wisdom he gave me early on was to be accepting of whatever gifts were provided to me by speakers at the various meetings I would attend over the years.

This came up after one meeting where the speaker went on and on and on about his drinking exploits. His talk was long, rambling and, frankly, not very interesting to me, as my journey was very different than his. After the meeting, I told my sponsor what I thought, as I judged the speaker not to have been very good. He looked at me knowingly and said that it was important to accept each person's story as their own. He explained that a large part of the AA program was about acceptance. Acceptance of what brought us to the meetings, of what we had done and of how we were, each in our own way, trying to get healthy.

He ended the lesson by suggesting that when speakers went on too long or might not have a great speaking style, I could at the very least see it as them giving me the gifts of patience and acceptance. Once again, the power of the Serenity Prayer came to mind, as it tells us to accept the things we cannot change—like a speaker who goes on too long.

Slowly, I began to assimilate the lessons I was learning in meetings and via discussions with my sponsor, and to leverage them both at work and home. Again, it's not like I immediately went from extremely unhealthy to extremely healthy. Not at all. However, the transformation was beginning.

•   •   •

"I'm not surprised. Your dad was an alcoholic, too."

That was my mother's response when I finally told my parents that I was in the AA program. She went on to explain that when I was young and had thought Dad was working late all those evenings, he was actually out drinking. I was shocked by the revelation that my father also had a drinking problem. He certainly hid it well (I guess the apple doesn't fall far from the tree) and had always been there for us.

Initially, I hadn't been planning to confess to my parents my own alcohol addiction, but a few days earlier I was speaking to my brother, Gary, and I shared with him what was going on. I told him I was getting help, including going to AA meetings, but that I didn't want to burden Mom and Dad with all my problems. The unspoken truth was that I was afraid of how they would look at me—failing again in life. But Gary urged me to tell our parents, saying, correctly, that they deserved to know.

Mom continued, saying that Dad didn't need AA, as he solved his problem by "getting down on his knees and praying." While it wasn't said, the implication was that, in her opinion, I didn't need AA, just pray to God and everything would be OK. Sure, I believe in God too, but I knew that I needed AA to truly get better.

In some respects, the knowledge of Dad's alcoholism might help to explain some things in my life. Was my addiction nature or nurture? Maybe some of both? I read somewhere that children of alcoholics have a 50 percent chance of becoming alcoholics themselves. I'm not sure if that is based on solid evidence, but it seems to make sense.

One critical thing I did learn for sure, though, was that no matter my family of origin, or the history of alcoholism in my family, no one was to "blame" for the person I became—other than me. I made this bed, and now it was time to lie in it. It was up to me to work hard, get the help I needed and strive to become the person I wanted to be; a person much more like that innocent, giving, loving young boy I grew up as.

•   •   •

Lise and I continued to seek counselling, both individually and as a couple. The couple sessions were especially hard, as I was always on the defensive, still believing that I was being attacked by both Lise and the counsellor(s). I knew that I was the person who needed to change the most, that I needed to get healthy, but I continued to judge that I wasn't the only one to blame here. It was likely 95 percent my "fault" that our marriage was in trouble, but nonetheless, I wanted to hear Lise accept at least some of the blame. In fairness, she did this, numerous times. However, in my mind, which was still very muddled and judgemental, it was never enough. It was not a lack of her speaking the words but a lack of my ability, and I suppose willingness at the time, to listen to them.

She was so quick to get angry at me now and, of course, I responded with anger of my own. We were in this vicious circle that started with blame, anger, guilt and accusations and, over time, was followed by regret, apologies and, eventually, some form of forgiveness. While I was trying to get healthy, the weight of this seemingly never-ending cycle continued to wear us both down. There were certainly times when I thought we would all be better off if I left her and we lived separately. I'm sure she had similar thoughts, and perhaps even took steps to prepare for that possibility.

When things got especially dark, I mentally explored more permanent options. Maybe it would be better if I wasn't around at all. If I wasn't even alive. I realize today that when I got "down" like that (as I preferred to think of it), I was actually in the middle of a depression, which sometimes included suicidal ideation. I would put on a brave face to the outside world, but when alone or with my family, I would sometimes withdraw totally—sometimes for hours, sometimes for days at a time.

I remember one day when we decided to go for a family walk in a forest south of Ottawa. It was supposed to be a fun time, but for some reason I can't explain, my mood turned dark and I mentally withdrew from Lise and the boys. She tried to talk to me, to get me to open up, but it was like I was in two different worlds simultaneously. I knew she and the boys were there, but at the same time, I felt so deeply alone, sad and empty. It was as if I were a zombie, unable to respond to her or our children, who I am sure were frightened by what they were watching.

I just walked and walked and walked. I thought about what a terrible person I was for having treated them all so poorly (and was, ironically, unable to recognize that I was doing so again at that very moment). I thought about how they would all be better off without me. But if I were to just leave home, the situation would only get worse because there would be even less money for them to live on.

No, the better solution in my mind at that moment was for me to kill myself. Everyone would be happier, and at least Lise would get money from the insurance. And if I could figure out a way to do it at work, a way that did not look like suicide, like driving my police car at high speed into a concrete abutment, then she would also get my salary and benefits until our youngest son was done university. I had no idea if that's how things worked but, in the depths of my despair, that's what I thought.

A few hours later, I started to come out of the darkness and Lise and the boys were still there with me, trying to get me to communicate. I opened up a little bit (nothing about the suicidal ideations) and told them that I was sorry. Daddy was just tired and needed to go home to sleep.

This was not the last time I had these thoughts, and I came very close to acting on them on several occasions. I still had more valleys of despair to navigate.

• • •

In the early years of my healing journey, it was often the case of one step forward and two steps back. Progress was slow and halting as a recovering addict (and as the saying goes, we are recovering forever—there is no "cure" for the disease of alcoholism); but I was gradually

learning how to put one foot in front of the other on the path to sobriety and reconciliation.

Another helpful thing I learned in AA was the acronym HALT,
which stands for hungry, angry, lonely or tired. As I was becoming more aware of myself and learning more from AA, my sponsor,
various councillors and my own research, I came to understand that
HALT was an early warning system of sorts, something I could rely
on to help me in my recovery. Any one of these symptoms—hunger,
anger, loneliness or tiredness—could cause me to relapse or, in my
case, start down the path towards depression. And if I allowed myself
to suffer from a combination of some or, God forbid, all of them at the
same time, then I was going to be in serious trouble.

Some people call alcoholics selfish, and that can certainly be true
when we are in the grips of our addiction. However, there is also a
sort of healthy selfishness in a recovering addict which I equate with
what we are told during airplane pre-flight briefings: "Put your mask
on first then help others who are travelling with you and need assistance." We can't help them if we don't look after ourselves first.

I needed—and still need—to look after myself first in recovery. If
I am hungry, I need to eat. If angry, I must use the tools I was taught
to manage that anger. If lonely, I need to talk to someone. If tired,
I need to sleep. Sounds selfish I know but, if you think about it, it
makes perfect sense. The only way I could be a good husband, father,
worker, boss or friend was to look after myself first. I was slowly
learning to do that—one day at a time.

Chapter 12
Begin with the End in Mind

As you might have noticed, I'm a big fan of Stephen Covey, the famous, and much too early deceased, author and motivational speaker. His seminal book, *The 7 Habits of Highly Effective People*, has been instrumental in my life since the early 1990s when I first read it. I've read the book multiple times now, with each reading revealing new layers and additional insights that I've sought to apply to every aspect of my life. I've also recommended the book to hundreds of people, even buying it for our children and a few others, in the hope that they, too, might find it useful in both their personal and professional lives.

After starting my recovery, I took the time to read the book again and was struck by so many new ideas and concepts. It was almost like my eyes were now open to additional secrets or "habits" that I was unable, or unwilling, to perceive before. Covey's second habit (to me, they are more principles than habits) is to "Begin with the end in mind." In that chapter, he asks readers to picture their own funeral and to think about what they hope people might say during the eulogies. Sounds like a simple exercise, but wow, can it bring up some heavy thoughts and feelings!

What did I want Lise, our children, my family and my friends to say about me at my funeral, I wondered. Would they say I was a kind, loving, respectful and gentle husband and father? Would they say I was a good and generous brother? An outstanding friend who was always there when someone needed help?

No, at this stage, if I was truly being honest with myself, they would say (or at least they'd be thinking) that I was a selfish, self-centred, egotistical and angry man. A man who was abusive towards his wife and constantly mean and demanding towards his children. A man whose "me first" attitude was evident to co-workers; a son and brother who only looked after his own needs. In Alcoholics Anonymous, we are taught that the first step is admitting that we have a problem. Well, I was now admitting to myself, for the first time, that the person I had become over the first thirty-nine years of my life was not the person I wanted people to be talking about at my funeral.

One of my favourite movies of all time is *It's a Wonderful Life*, starring Jimmy Stewart and Donna Reed. There's a scene in the movie where the main character, George Bailey, played by Stewart, is standing on a bridge in the middle of a snowstorm, considering taking his own life. An angel, Clarence, with a bit of help from Saint Peter, temporarily grants George his wish to have never lived. He has a chance to relive key moments of his life—with one difference. He is not "alive" during the re-enactment and so is able to see the impact of him not living on his family, friends and even their little town.

George stands on the bridge, crying, now realizing what his not being alive would do to everyone he loved. How all their lives were truly enriched by his life. He is, self-admittedly, not a religious man. However, in that moment of desperation, he cries out:

I want to live again.
I want to live again.

I want to live again.
Please, God, let me live again.

I watch that movie every year. Sometimes with my family if they are willing, and sometimes I watch alone. I cry every time I watch it. I'm crying as I write these words.

I did not want to die with my wife, boys, family and friends thinking that I was such a terrible person. I wanted to change. To become the person that I once was, and who I hoped I could be again. Now that I knew what I wanted, I had to figure out how I would make this transformation real. Unfortunately, wanting something and getting it are two entirely different things. As I was to learn, there would still be many more descents into dark valleys on the journey to the mountaintop of a loving, respectful and healthy life.

Some of the darkest days still lay ahead.

•   •   •

Alcoholism is a disease. It's listed as "Alcohol Use Disorder" in the *Diagnostic and Statistical Manual of Mental Disorders*. The first time I ever heard that was at an AA meeting. Not in any of my training as a police officer or during my then almost twenty years in patrol, on detective teams or as a sergeant or staff sergeant. Frankly, even if I did hear the words in my professional life, I would have laughed. Alcoholism a disease? No way. I believed that alcoholics were a bunch of lazy, useless, undisciplined and selfish guys (I always thought alcoholics were almost all men, something I now know is entirely inaccurate) who have given up on themselves and their families. I had no time for them and thought they just needed to straighten up and fly right.

For the first time, in AA, I learned that the American Medical Association had defined alcoholism as a disease in 1991, upgrading it from what they had previously called an "illness." They define it as follows:

> *Alcoholism or alcohol dependence is defined by the American Medical Association (AMA) as "a primary, chronic disease with genetic, psychosocial, and environmental factors influencing its development and manifestations."*[8]

My attitude towards alcoholism was, like most biases, based on limited understanding and supported by my "confirmation bias" whereby I only looked at, and for, things that supported my position at the time. All the drunks (or "rubbies," as we used to call them) that I had picked up over the years, especially when walking the beat downtown or assigned to Car 808, the Ottawa Police drunk truck, fit the mental description I provided a few paragraphs ago. The only "drunk" I knew about in my extended family was a great uncle whom I don't remember ever meeting. Drunks were, in my mind, not professional or successful. They were losers.

I've already described how significantly my attitude and perceptions changed between my first AA meeting on February 1, 1996, and the second one, Alta Vista Open Door, on February 2. Of course, nothing was different about the people attending those two meetings; in fact, a number of the same people attended both. It was my perception, my beliefs and my attitude that had changed over the twenty-four hours in between.

Attitudes follow beliefs. My eyes were opening to the truths about alcoholics and alcoholism. I was learning that the people attending AA came from all walks of life. All backgrounds, races, religions and,

---

8. medical-dictionary.thefreedictionary.com/alcoholism

surprisingly for me, sexes. While there were typically more men at the meetings I went to, there were lots of women as well. Their stories were no different, for the most part, than the men's.

I learned that there are women-only meetings and others, called "Nomad" meetings, for people who need to be extremely discreet about their attendance. All AA meetings are confidertial, with the warning voiced at every meeting: "What you see here, what you hear here, when you leave here, let it stay here." That being said, some people, like celebrities or politicians, just can't take the chance of going to a "regular" AA meeting. As a result, they created the Nomad approach. I've never been to a Nomad meeting but know a few people who attend.

I now know that some of the most famous, most successful, people in the world are recovering alcoholics. Presidents, prime ministers, doctors, lawyers, even clergy, as well as cops and criminals. There is no such thing as a "profile" of what an alcoholic person looks like or where they work. If there is a profile, it likely relates to their family history, upbringing or personality type, not their race, sex or career.

While my attitudes and belief systems towards all forms of addiction have evolved (people addicted to narcotics are no better or worse than those addicted to alcohol), I'm sorry to say that, for the most part, our society's views have not. Major negative stereotypes about alcoholics abound and, despite all the wonderful work by many to reduce the stigma associated with addiction and mental health, alcoholics are still viewed in a negative light.

I've witnessed this myself numerous times over the years since starting my recovery. Once, I was out for a drink (typically sparkling water) with several senior police officers. One of them, a chief of police, was drinking pretty heavily, and when someone mentioned something about alcoholism, he said something like, "Those fuckers need to take themselves less seriously and have a drink. That'll solve their problems."

Of course, he had no idea that he was sitting beside one of "those fuckers." Over the following two and a half decades I rarely told any-one that I was an alcoholic. I couldn't take the chance that they might use it against me or my family. Society was not and, in my opinion, still is not ready to accept that alcoholism is a disease and that those who suffer from it need support and compassion, not derision and scorn.

•   •   •

So here I was in late 1996, now officially, and by my own admission, a drunk. How was I going to deal with that label and balance the reality of it with my previous ideas of what it meant? The answer, as when debunking most biases, was to learn more about alcoholism, what it was and how best to deal with it.

The first source of this knowledge came from a book my sponsor gave me called the "Big Book." Its actual title is *Alcoholics Anonymous: The Story of How More Than One Hundred Men Have Recovered from Alcoholism,*[9] written by Bill W. and first published in 1939. Amazingly, the Big Book is one of the best-selling books of all time with over thirty million copies sold!

In the book, Bill writes about both his and Dr. Bob's history with alcohol as well as the stories of several other men (again, the idea of women suffering from this disease was pretty much unheard of then). There are sections on the Twelve Steps (as previously outlined) and something read at many, but not all, AA meetings called the Twelve Promises. As you can see below, these promises outline what

---

9. en.wikipedia.org/wiki/The_Big_Book-Alcoholics_Anonymous

an alcoholic can expect if they commit to the program.

The Twelve Promises[10]

1. We are going to know a new freedom and a new happiness.
2. We will not regret the past nor wish to shut the door on it.
3. We will comprehend the word serenity.
4. We will know peace.
5. No matter how far down the scale we have gone, we will see how our experience can benefit others.
6. That feeling of uselessness and self-pity will disappear.
7. We will lose interest in selfish things and gain interest in our fellows.
8. Self-seeking will slip away.
9. Our whole attitude and outlook on life will change.
10. Fear of people and economic insecurity will leave us.
11. We will intuitively know how to handle situations which used to baffle us.
12. We will suddenly realize that God is doing for us what we could not do for ourselves.

Are these extravagant promises? We think not. They are being fulfilled among us—sometimes quickly, sometimes slowly. They will always materialize if we work for them.

Truth be told, achieving these twelve promises is not quite that simple. It takes a lot of work to shake deeply entrenched thoughts and feelings. I'll talk more in a chapter titled "Today" about whether and

---

10. www.aacle.org/what-is-aa/twelve-promises/

how these "promises" have been met during my journey. For now, suffice it to say that at that very early stage of my recovery, they provided me, and Lise, with a great deal of hope and a vision for what the future might hold—if I worked hard and committed to getting healthy.

•   •   •

Hockey slowly began to play an ever-increasing role in our family. When our oldest son, Jonny, turned eight in 1996, he asked if he could start to play organized hockey. After discussing it, Lise and I signed him up. That fall, I took him to his first tryout at the Orleans Sportsplex. He was excited to get onto the ice with the other kids and to show me how he could skate.

He was clearly behind most of the kids, many of whom had already played in the Orleans Minor Hockey Association for three or even four years. As Jonny "skated" (more like walked) around the rink, I was happy for him and proud to see how well he was doing, especially with him not having had any lessons. I had been a goalie for most of my hockey-playing days. Back then, goalies were only expected to go forward and backward, left or right and up or down. I was (and am) a terrible skater and can still barely do crossovers.

A few minutes later, the coach leading the tryout blew his whistle and had everyone stop, although it took Jonny a few seconds as he worked hard to stop without falling. The coach then told everyone to turn around and skate backwards. My first thought was, *Shit, I never taught him how to skate backwards.* Sure enough, there he was, standing on the opposite blue line, his feet shuffling straight backwards and forwards and never moving off the line. Some of the other parents were pointing at him and laughing (my first introduction to how mean-spirited some hockey parents can be). I was sitting there thinking how upset Jonny must be and how much I had let him down. *What kind of terrible parent doesn't teach a Canadian kid how to skate?*

As the tryout progressed, the children were getting tired; many started crying and asked their parents if they could leave the ice. But Jonny kept working hard and attempting to do whatever the coaches were asking him and the other kids to do. After it was over, I was expecting him to want to quit hockey, but instead he came off the ice with the biggest smile asking, "Dad, can we go public skating today? I need to learn how to skate backwards!" (Clearly, he got his positive attitude and sense of adventure from his mother.) I was so proud of him.

Over the years, I ended up coaching all three boys at various levels of minor hockey (and softball). As a result, I had the opportunity to spend hundreds of wonderful, fulfilling hours with them. More about all that later, but in the early years especially, hockey provided me an avenue to focus more on our children and a little bit less on me and the challenges I was facing.

• • •

Although I was beginning to get healthy, both Lise and I continued to struggle in our own way. As I said earlier, it's not like you walk in the doors of a program like AA, or go to a marriage counsellor, and everything magically improves. Not at all. Like most other things, it takes time. And more. The saying "time heals all wounds" might be true—but only if the people involved work hard on the issues and the hurt that created the wounds. For me to have apologized numerous times was not enough. Lise also needed to see that my actions, my behaviours, were changing; that the anger, shouting, demeaning and disrespect were gone.

I wish I could say that happened right from the get-go, but it would not be true. This is not an excuse at all, but there was still a great deal of stress in our lives, in our marriage. Money continued to be tight, especially since I had become a staff sergeant. While my base salary was higher with the promotion, my ability to make overtime and court time had pretty much vanished—and that's where the extra money had been coming from over the past few years.

Work on both the B&E Squad, which continued to excel, and the expert system project, which was moving forward nicely, were rewarding but also extremely demanding. The fact that I had cancelled my university courses certainly helped reduce the stress on our relationship and, while disappointed to have given them up, I knew it had been the correct decision. However, resentments—an absolute killer for alcoholics—continued to build, likely in both of us but certainly for me. All of us feel resentment from time to time, but for me, and apparently for many suffering from the same problems, it was always bubbling just under the surface.

Resentment about why Lise didn't understand everything I had done for her and the boys. Resentment about her not going back to work full-time and helping more with the finances (despite us both agreeing that her staying home was the best thing for our little family). Resentment about me giving up my university courses while, at the same time, she was going back to school to finish her undergraduate degree (also something we had both discussed and agreed to). These are just three of many resentments that would regularly pop into my brain, which was constantly spinning out of control like a hamster on a wheel. At the same time, Lise was, understandably, struggling with true forgiveness.

Stephen Covey uses a wonderful metaphor when discussing relationships. He talks about our "emotional bank accounts." When we do things that are kind, generous and loving for our partner, we are making a deposit into this metaphorical bank account. Over time, the account grows and becomes healthy. From time to time in a healthy relationship, one of the partners does something that hurts the other. This is a form of withdrawal from that bank account. If there is a surplus of deposits that have been built up over time, then this withdrawal, assuming it is not too large (such as an affair), won't empty the account and it can be relatively easy to get back on track, assuming that there has been an appropriate and heartfelt apology, a lasting change of behaviour and true forgiveness by the slighted partner.

However, and this was our situation, if there have been frequent withdrawals over a long period of time, perhaps perceived as never-ending, then the bank account becomes depleted. Even despite the odd deposit, something like, "Honey, I know we can't afford it, but let's go out for a nice romantic dinner," typically offered up after a fight. Eventually, with more withdrawals than deposits, there's no money (emotional capital) left in the account. It is in the "red" and way past any overdraft capacity that might have been there before all the negative behaviours started years ago.

That's where Lise was now with our relationship. First and foremost, she didn't truly believe that I was going to get healthy. Why should she? I had promised so many times before that I would stop overreacting, getting excessively angry and becoming verbally and emotionally abusive.

"Triggering" has become a well-known concept in today's world. Back then we, or at least I, had never heard of it. Well, I can tell you that when I started getting angry all over again, Lise was triggered big time. Emotionally, and almost instantaneously, she went right back to the worst days, the days that led her to getting help and eventually asking me to leave. Her immediate and visceral response was, "Hell no, I'm not going back to that bullshit."

Another way to look at it was that she was leveraging the lessons she had learned in Al-Anon and was, appropriately, setting her boundaries. That was good and positive and necessary. However, her ability to deal with minor disagreements and arguments had been greatly diminished due to her emotional bank account having been empty for so long. What would have been a minor disagreement when we were first married was, under our current circumstances, an absolute "no-fly zone" for her. She was unwilling, even unable, to deal with any bullshit at all.

Both of us were now emotionally spent. We needed help to find our way back to a healthy, loving and respectful relationship. Yes, I was the alcoholic with a wide range of mental health issues and was primarily the one who needed to change. However, Lise was hurt, sad, physically tired and emotionally drained to the core. While the kind of support she needed was different, there was no doubt we needed professional help, both as individuals and as a couple.

• • •

The following year, 1997, was a year of great transition for both of us. Lise went back to school (St. Paul's University, part of the University of Ottawa) to complete her undergraduate degree. Many of her courses were around psychology, counselling, theology and philosophy. These had always been areas that interested her, but I'm sure our circumstances provided additional motivation to study these subjects, in the hope of gaining further insights into our dynamic and possibly even learning new tools that might help her and our relationship.

For me, the expert system project had come to a very interesting fork in the road. The National Research Council (NRC), the agency funding and leading the research, was all about commercialization, taking the lessons learned and the intellectual property (IP) from projects it was funding and leveraging them financially, typically through the creation of a company by those who had done the research or by selling or assigning the IP for a predetermined period to another party or parties.

The primary researcher on our expert systems project had no interest in trying to start a company, so the NRC started a process to identify the best company to take the intellectual property (things like the "rules" we had developed) and turn it into a new product that could be sold across Canada and around the world. The revenues from those sales could not only create wealth for the selected company but could also generate potential royalties both for the NRC and, to a much lesser extent, the researchers (not me, as I was not an employee of the NRC).

It was a fascinating process, and I was happy to be invited to participate. Several companies submitted proposals, most of them quite well-known in the police technology space. However, the successful bidder was a "virtual" company, in the sense that it had no buildings or employees at the outset. They were going to start from scratch and take the ideas, concepts and rules we had created and best practices we had developed and run with them to develop innovative software products for the policing community. This exciting Canadian start-up company was called InvestigAide.

A few months after InvestigAide was selected, the president called me and asked if we could meet. He explained that things were going very well but they had one major problem. When they met with police agencies to talk about what they were developing, there was a major gap in their ability to explain it in terms the police leaders and investigators could understand. He asked me if I would be willing to take a leave of absence and come work for them as their general manager. It would mean leaving the police service for a year, but I would be returning with an entirely new set of knowledge, skills and abilities. As a start-up, they didn't have money to pay big salaries but could afford to pay me what I was then earning as a staff sergeant. They would also "buy back" any pension time that I lost so that I could still retire as planned at the end of my career.

While there was no financial gain in this proposal, I was immediately interested. My desire to be constantly evolving and learning (and feeding my ego) had certainly not diminished, so this looked like a cool opportunity. After discussing it with Lise, I drafted a memo and sent it to the chief for his consideration. A few weeks later, I was called up to the chief's office, where he told me that he had approved the leave of absence and had signed the "General Order" that morning (something I have thanked him for many times over the years).

That day, another new chapter in our lives began.

•   •   •

Lise and I continued to seek help, with both of us seeing counsellors on an individual basis. We would also go together from time to time, but it didn't seem like we were making much headway. We were still living together, but there was a constant level of friction, and it was easy to move from that into an argument.

One of the places we went for help was called Serenity Renewal for Families. Sister Louise, who has since passed away, was an absolute little firecracker and refused to let me spout any bullshit. She called it as she saw it and was relentless in her ability to cut through the shit and get to the heart of the matter. There's no doubt in my mind that Lise, AA, my sponsor, Sister Louise and Serenity Renewal were all critical components on my road to recovery. Put more bluntly, they saved my life.

Sister Louise and others, including my sponsor, recommended that I participate in a two-week live-in program in Elliot Lake, Ontario, where there's a recovery facility called Camillus Centre, part of St. Joseph's Hospital. I wasn't keen on the idea. I would have to take two weeks of my annual leave to seek treatment, which irked me. Also, I was afraid of what I might find out about myself and what else I might have to give up. *Haven't I done enough yet? Why is everyone telling me I need to do more? Will this shit never end?*

While I had committed to AA and getting help, I thought this was going too far. Additional resentments started to build up in my mind, and my critical defence systems were on high alert. *What'll happen there? Who else will be there? What will I be expected to do, to share?* The bottom line was that I felt afraid and angry that this was being thrust upon me. At the same time, deep down I knew that if our marriage was to survive and if I was to get better, I needed to follow everyone's advice and submit myself to this level of intense therapy. I called the centre, registered and was given a date to show up.

No turning back now.

•   •   •

I took two weeks off from work and, with a huge amount of anxiety and trepidation, set off on the seven-hour drive to Elliot Lake. Seven hours alone, especially once you have kids, is pretty rare. It certainly gave me time to think about everything that had transpired over the past few years. Once again, I was asking myself what had happened to me. *Why's my life so fucked up? Where's God in all of this?*

As a child, I had been taught that we had free will. Even though, in the Catholic religion at least, God is "all-knowing and all-seeing," He (and God was always portrayed as a male) wouldn't stop us if we were going off track. We could make our own decisions, good or bad, righteous or sinful. I was also raised to believe that God is all-powerful and punishes evil. Fire and brimstone. Thunder and lightning bolts crashing down on sinners. In the Catholic religion, there are seven "mortal" (major) sins, often called the Seven Deadly Sins. They are pride, greed, wrath, envy, lust, gluttony and sloth. There was no doubt in my mind that I was guilty of a number of them. I was a sinner. *What did that mean for me?*

The good news is that the church gives us a way out through the "Sacrament of Reconciliation," commonly known as confession. Catholics believe that mortal sins can be absolved only by an ordained priest. I had gone to confession several times over the past couple of years and admitted to the priest what I had done. Although they had absolved (forgiven) me, I couldn't help but think that God was still, justifiably, pissed at me, and that there was another punishment waiting down the road. In my mind, God was about sin and punishment and, most of all, guilt. I had lived in a constant state of guilt for years and nothing was taking that away. Not for what I had done. It was a very long, miserable drive to Elliot Lake with all these thoughts rattling around in my head.

Upon arrival at Camillus Centre, I checked in and soon realized that this wasn't going to be like staying at a nice five-star hotel. The rooms were even more spartan than I'd had at the Ontario Police College. The chores they expected us to do and the rules we were to follow, such as never leaving the property, were, I felt, ridiculous. Here I was, a staff sergeant with a major Canadian police service, and I was being treated like a criminal.

I almost left the first day.

The other residents participating in this fourteen-day recovery program were from all walks of life and were mostly male, although there were some women. There were multiple people there on a court order, having been convicted during criminal trials for various offences and told this was part of their sentence. They had no choice but to attend. If they left or were booted out, they would be going back to jail. Some of them might have preferred that.

Everyone had chores or tasks assigned to them. Mine was to do the garbage and sweep up the kitchen and dining hall after others had done the dishes. I felt angry at everything that I was experiencing. Angry at Lise for forcing me to come to this fucking place. Angry about all the fucking rules. Angry about why my life was such a fucking mess.

I was running quite a bit at that time and wanted to get some of my anger and frustration (just another word for pent-up anger) out of my system by going running. On the first day, I followed the rules and ran only around the building, over and over and over again. I kept looking down the street, which was only about two hundred metres long, thinking, *What the hell does it matter if I run to the end of the street and back? At least that way everyone else doesn't have to watch me run circles around the building.*

At the end of our sessions the next day, I had an hour of free time, so I went for another run. This time, I thought, *Fuck it*, left the property and ran to the end of the street and back multiple times. It felt great to break the rules. Until I was told to go see the administrator. She told me that she was considering kicking me out of the program for breaking the rules. I couldn't believe it, and I argued with her. I told her what I did for a living and that I was not here like some criminal, I was special.

She smiled, clearly seeing through all my bullshit (because she'd been dealing with liars and bullshitters for decades) and quickly set me straight. I could either fully commit to the program and everything it entailed, including doing chores and not leaving the grounds, or I could leave.

I took a few moments to think about what she was saying and to think about what I would be losing if I left. I would lose Lise and the boys for sure. I might lose my policing career if I started drinking again. I might even lose my life if things kept spiralling down.

I've got no choice. I've got to commit. I realized that I needed to get rid of the "King Baby I" attitude they had spoken of so often at my AA meetings. That's when alcoholics fall into the trap of consistently thinking of themselves with a "Poor me" attitude, resulting in negative behaviours that flow from that mental trap. *Fuck it! I guess it's time to put up or shut up.*

I stayed and, in many ways, that program transformed my life. The two most profound ways it changed my life were in how I found a "new" God and how God and I actually communicated one day.

I was in a private therapy session with our primary counsellor. We were talking about my "family of origin"; essentially, how I was raised, my religious beliefs, my siblings and so on. When we started talking about religion, she asked me to describe God. I told her what I had been raised to believe and said that, in my mind, God was all-powerful and all about sin, punishment and guilt. I described God using the thunder-and-lightning-bolt metaphor, as that was how I pictured Him.

She quietly, and with a sense of confidence I was not used to, said to me, "You know you can choose a different God, right?"

I stared at her like she had three heads, asking, "What do you mean, I can choose a different God? That's crazy!"

She smiled and told me, "No, it wasn't crazy." She explained that I didn't have to believe in a God who was all about sin, guilt and punishment. I could choose a God who was all about love, forgiveness and acceptance.

I sat there, dumbfounded. *Is this true? Can I just choose another God? Can God be gentle and kind and accepting of me and all my weaknesses, my mistakes, my faults?* While I knew that this new God would also hold me to account and want me to be the very best version of myself that I could be, there was no doubt in my mind that I wanted a different kind of relationship with God. I didn't want to feel guilty all the time. I wanted to feel love, forgiveness and acceptance.

Yep—new God for me, please!

Partway through the second week of the program, things were going well. I was learning a great deal about alcoholism, its underlying causes, various ways I could help myself get better and tools that I could use when things were not going well. We were also taught some Indigenous concepts, either by staff or by other residents.

One day, I was walking around the building with another resident and pulled a small piece of cedar spray (the tip of a branch) from a cedar tree (called the "Tree of God" by Hindus). I love the smell of cedar and have always found it a kind of cleansing scent. I would often take some and smell it while hunting or walking in the woods. The other resident stopped, pulled a pouch from their pocket and sprinkled something in the area of the tree, mumbling some words. When they finished, I asked what they had done. They explained that whenever we take something from Mother Nature (their higher power), we need to give something back. In this case, it was some sweet tobacco that they kept with them for these kinds of situations. While I never took up the practice of carrying sweet tobacco, every time I take something from nature now, like another spray of cedar, I thank God for nature's bounty and for my having the opportunity to enjoy it.

The second profound thing that happened to me at Camillus Centre was that God spoke to me.

Directly. As in, I heard His voice.

Yeah, I know, hard to believe right? I've only ever told this story to a few people, and most of them, except for Lise, smile and tell me, "That's great Lance," all the while thinking I'm crazy.

One day, we were given an assignment to go out into the forest beside the centre, find a tree and hug it. Now, I had been a cop for a fairly long time by this point and had come to view environmentalists as "tree huggers." The idea of actually hugging a tree was pretty out there for me. Having said that, I was now in a much better place mentally and no longer feeling angry and resentful about this recovery process, this journey. I was accepting of it and all that it entailed. So, if they wanted me to go hug a tree, then that's what I was going to do.

Everyone went into the forest and separated so that we couldn't see or hear each other. Following the instructions, I took my time and thought about what kind of tree I wanted to select for hugging. Big? Small? Medium-sized? Cedar? Birch? Elm? Oak? Pine was out because it would hurt and I would get all sticky with the tree gum.

While searching, I was also thinking and praying to my "new" God. Not to help me find the right tree, because that would just be silly. *God, please help me. Help me find this serenity everyone is talking about. Help Lise and the boys forgive me. Help me, Lord.* I don't think I considered self-forgiveness at that time. That possibility was still far down the line, and I still don't know if it will ever truly come. I guess I was mostly praying that I could find God's love and feel the warmth and comfort that it would provide.

I found a nice big oak tree. It was too large for me to put my arms all the way around it but, for some reason, I knew this was the tree. I took a deep breath and embraced it, stretching my arms as far as they would go. I held it gently and tried to become one with it. I started praying again, and then, out of nowhere, I heard a voice as if it were right beside me. No, it was above me, saying, "I am here." Part of me was shocked, and another, deeper, part of me felt only warmth and calmness. I continued to pray, and again heard, "I am here."

A few minutes later, I let go of the tree and wondered if that had actually happened. I was certainly not drunk or on drugs. I wasn't hallucinating. Yes, I acknowledged—I had heard God speak to me. Not a conversation. Nothing miraculous. Just, "I am here."

I wrote about the experience in my journal, something we were encouraged to do, but I didn't tell anyone else at the time. I thought they would think I was crazy and possibly put me into another part of the hospital where I wouldn't be able to get out—also known as the psych ward!

• • •

The two-week program came to a close, and we all went our separate ways. I took the long drive back to Orleans, and it was a far more peaceful trip. My anger, resentments and frustration had all been replaced with a new acceptance and a desire to continue my recovery with much more love, respect and kindness towards Lise, the boys and all the others who would cross my path going forward.

I knew, both intuitively and because they had warned us, that there were still many challenges to face. This was not a straight-line journey, from the depths of the valley of darkness to the peaks of the mountaintops of joy. No, there were more valleys to come, but at least I would be better equipped to get through them.

Unfortunately, I had no idea just how dark, lonely, despondent and utterly hopeless some of those valleys would become.

• • •

I got back home just in time to take Dominic to his first set of hockey tryouts. Having learned my lesson with Jonny, I had prepared Dominic much better for the event, and he could even skate backwards! It was wonderful to see him skating around the rink, fitting right in from the get-go. Dominic, like most children, had (has) qualities that come from both of his parents. In the social skills arena, though, he gets his outgoing, friendly nature from his mom. It didn't take long before he had a bunch of new friends, and it was great to see him continuing to grow in this area of his life. Years later, when Dominic got married, many of the guests at their wedding were friends he had met while playing hockey over the years. It truly was an amazing circle of life that began on that rink that day.

• • •

In the fall of 1997, I turned in my gun, my badge and all my use-of-force equipment to the quartermaster. It was, to say the least, a very strange feeling as I walked out of headquarters afterwards. The first time I hadn't been a cop in twenty years.

Being a police officer had been such a large part of my identity, as it is for most officers, that it was hard for me to separate work from non-work life. Everywhere I went I was constantly looking for threats, scanning licence plates to see if they looked abnormal and to be sure they had the correct licencing sticker on the top-right corner of the rear plate. When in a restaurant or at a bar, I always sat in a corner and faced the entrance. These and dozens of other small things wouldn't change just because I was no longer a cop (and they still haven't changed).

Going to work for a small Canadian start-up company was both exciting and scary. *Am I doing the right thing? Will there be negative impacts on my family and my career? Do I have what it takes to help lead this new company to success?* But it turned out that all my fears were unfounded.

It was a fascinating time as we worked together, travelling across Canada, the United States and the United Kingdom to attend meetings with police leaders and conferences such as the Canadian Association of Chiefs of Police and the International Association of Chiefs of Police. I learned an amazing amount during the two years of my InvestigAide leave of absence (I asked for an extension after the first year). That experience absolutely helped shape the rest of my career. Suffice it to say that they were two of the best professional years I've ever had.

Chapter 13
Welcome Back

A couple of months before it was time for me to return to the Ottawa Police, I arranged a meeting with the new deputy chief responsible for operations. This was the division I had been working in when I took the leave of absence, and I was hoping to go back there, ideally to my old job in the B&E Squad. It was a new deputy who had come from another agency to join the service. We had met a couple times while I was working for InvestigAide, and I'd found him to be extremely professional and a wonderful communicator.

He greeted me warmly in his office and, after we had caught up, he told me that he had other plans for me. He said he wanted to leverage all the exciting and innovative things I'd learned in the private sector and was going to create a new role for me and name me the Ottawa Police "technology champion." He wanted me to review all aspects of our technology and to find ways to utilize what we already owned, or purchase new tools, to improve our operational effectiveness and efficiency. He was giving me carte blanche to go where I wanted and do pretty much what I wanted throughout the police service—anything related to technology innovation.

Cool!

I asked who I would be reporting to and he immediately responded that it would be him. I pointed out that a staff sergeant reporting to a deputy chief was unusual and was likely going to create some internal political problems. He said he didn't care and that for me to have the best chance of success he needed to have my back.

We went together down to the second floor to meet with the superintendent of the Criminal Investigations Division, where my "substantive" position as the staff sergeant in the Break and Enter Squad belonged. The deputy chief told the superintendent what I would be doing. He had only one question: "Who does he report to?" When the deputy told him that it would be him, the deputy chief, the superintendent replied, "OK." That was the end of the conversation, and that superintendent didn't speak to me again for years.

Like I said, this was going to cause some internal political problems.

Despite that initial hiccup, my new job was fantastic, and I spent the next couple of years meeting with both sworn and civilian staff from throughout the service, asking questions and looking for better ways to use technology to help them do their jobs.

One of the first new technologies I purchased, for about $500, was a high-speed PDF scanner. Now, today that doesn't seem very innovative, but I can tell you it saved a lot of people massive amounts of time and effort. Back then, scanning a large document meant placing each page on a slow-speed scanner, page by page, sometimes taking hours to complete. The new device allowed folks to scan an entire document and create one PDF instead of hundreds of separate ones. Everyone loved the thing!

We also developed a plan for the first Ottawa Police Intranet that, once built, became the home page for all OPS members, with a wide range of resources now available at our fingertips. Again, I know that to today's readers, especially the younger ones, this sounds pretty old school. But for us, in the early 2000s, it was groundbreaking stuff and everyone was thrilled.

• • •

This role also provided me with the opportunity of a lifetime, the chance to join the prestigious Canadian Association of Chiefs of Police Informatics Committee (later called the Information & Communications Technology Committee). The deputy chief I reported to was a member, and he invited me to participate in their very first conference, which was held in 2000 in Cornwall.

One of the first things I noted about the committee was that there were few members and they were not leveraging technology very much themselves, with all meetings being held in person. I recommended that we open it up to other police technology leaders from across the country and hold meetings via teleconference, with face-to-face meetings being held less frequently. This would help agencies to reduce costs while allowing the committee to accomplish more.

Over time, this committee became one of the most productive and sought-after groups within the CACP committee structure. I had the opportunity to meet and work with many of Canada's leading police information management experts, including every RCMP CIO, for decades. We also interacted regularly with various chiefs of police who were on the CACP Board of Directors and with senior government officials who were involved in our various projects.

The lessons learned on this committee were numerous and long-lasting. One of the greatest takeaways was, as Covey would say, the importance of not only doing things right but, even more importantly, doing the right things. We had an opportunity to see the big picture, not only in Canada but, through our association with the International Association of Chiefs of Police, the worldwide landscape.

Stephen Covey was a wonderful storyteller, something that makes his book both easy to read and remember. One of his stories, or parables, is about a group of lumberjacks working in a jungle cutting and stacking trees. They are doing a fantastic job, and everything is going extremely well. Until one of them eventually climbs to the top of the tallest tree and looks around, yelling to his counterparts, "We're in the wrong jungle!"

Covey uses this story to talk about the difference between managers and leaders, but I've always thought it was also highly relevant to the concept of thinking strategically and looking for ways to improve via enhanced governance, standard-setting and national-level planning (not federal-level planning; there's a major difference between the two in Canada).

I ended up staying on the committee for close to twenty years, and it led to much of my post-retirement success.

•   •   •

In early 2001, I was speaking to my boss, who had become the chief of police, about a project we were working on. At the end of the conversation, he told me that he believed it was time for me to enter the competitive application process to become an inspector. I let him know that I was very happy as a staff sergeant and was continuing to enjoy the role I was now playing as the Ottawa Police technology champion. He looked at me and said something to the effect of, "I'd like it if you'd enter into the process." I smiled, and said, "Of course, sir."

At that level, the selection process is quite detailed and onerous. However, I did well and was ranked as one of the top candidates at its conclusion. A few months later, I was promoted to inspector and named as one of six Ottawa Police Service duty inspectors, otherwise known as incident commanders. This role was first created after several high-profile incidents in the National Capital Region, where the traditional process of rotating regular inspectors as incident commanders had led to less than positive results. The majority of the rotating inspectors were, in all likelihood, great at their day-to-day jobs. However, they didn't have the training, nor in some cases the personality traits, required to safely and effectively manage highly complex and dangerous critical incidents.

Of all the postings I had during my career, being a duty inspector was one of the most fun and rewarding. We were in charge of all major incidents, such as tactical calls, major missing-person searches and VIP visits to the city. We trained and worked closely with the various specialty squads like Tactical, Negotiators, Public Order (aka Riot Squads) and, of course, all aspects of patrol and investigative services.

We were fortunate to be able to train not only with our own excellent teams but also with external partners such as the Canadian Armed Forces. Ottawa is home to one of the world's leading elite special forces teams, located at Dwyer Hill Training Centre in the city's southwest end. This team, known as Joint Task Force 2 (JTF2), is staffed by some of the best-trained special forces operators in the world. Working with them was a highlight in my career, as their level of planning and professionalism was off the charts, and something for all of us to attempt to emulate.

In one training exercise, which I am not at liberty to discuss in any detail, I had the chance to observe their commander briefing the troops just before they executed their mission, a major exercise in Ottawa's south end. The hair still goes up on the back of my neck when I think of that briefing, which left me with absolute confidence that, if ever needed, our "backup" was both close by and unbelievably capable of coming to save the day!

Two events stand out in my time as a duty inspector. The first was 9/11 and the second was the visit of President George W. Bush to Ottawa in 2004.

I was working out on the morning of September 11, 2001, in the basement gym of the police building on Greenbank Road in Nepean, when someone came in and told us to turn on the TV. We watched the horrific events unfold for a few minutes, and then I quickly showered and headed downtown to our headquarters building on Elgin Street for what we all knew would be a very long day.

I was assigned by the chief to represent the service at the City of Ottawa's Emergency Operations Centre. This is where all city department heads, including the mayor as required, work together in a crisis situation to gather information, develop plans and ensure those plans are properly executed. We learned early on that all planes were being told to land immediately, so there were going to be massive requirements for housing, food, logistics and so on. Although this was not the responsibility of the police service, we were certainly critical in supporting the operation.

Due to a lack of communication by our federal partners, it was not until much later in the day that we found out the Government of Canada had decided no planes would be allowed anywhere near Ottawa. As a result, all the planning for accommodating thousands of additional people had been, in some respects, a waste of time. However, this kind of planning is never truly a waste; we learned a great deal that would be helpful in future events.

In late 2004, we learned with just two weeks' notice that President George W. Bush was going to be visiting Ottawa. Although his visit was going to last less than two days, the level of planning and support required was herculean.

As with all major events—like G8 (now G7) meetings, Summits of the Americas and various visits by what are known as Internationally Protected Persons, or IPPs—we used a "first seat" and "second seat" approach to planning. That is, a more experienced duty inspector is the incident commander (first seat), and a less experienced duty inspector is the deputy incident commander, or second seat. This structure does two things. First, it gives the less experienced inspector the chance to learn invaluable lessons right in the middle of major events. Second, it gives the primary incident commander a second set of eyes and ears to support their decision-making processes. Sometimes it's nice to walk away from the table and have a quiet, confidential chat with your counterpart to help ensure things are going well.

For President Bush's impending visit, I was named as the Ottawa Police Service's incident commander (first seat) and would be working closely with the RCMP and all our other policing partners from across Ontario who were kindly sending additional officers, mostly public-order teams, to support security at the event. I learned a great deal and reinforced previous learnings during this high-stress operation. First and foremost was the fact that good communications were critical. This will be no surprise to anyone who has ever been involved in managing critical incidents; communication is almost always one of the top issues identified during any after-action review. Secondly, we needed to get much better at information sharing among the various police services and our partner agencies.

I semi-jokingly tell people that the three most important words that an incident commander needs to know during a major event are "What's for lunch?" (technically four words, I know). Why? Because once an event starts, all the careful planning has already taken place;

all the right people are, hopefully, in the right roles; and then we simply need to rely on all our training to ensure that everything goes smoothly.

However, there is also a famous military saying, "No plan survives first contact with the enemy." While we certainly don't consider protestors as "the enemy," there's no doubt that there are usually a small number of them who attend these events only to disrupt the proceedings. Why else do they show up with Molotov cocktails (bottles filled with flammable fluids), slingshots with ball bearings and various other weapons? We can plan all we like for many contingencies, but we can never be certain what we will face or how we will need to adapt as the situation unfolds.

I made several mistakes during those two days, but everything went smoothly overall. I was very proud of the approximately two thousand officers and civilians who worked tirelessly to manage everyone's safety, particularly the president's. In the end, we heard the only words we wanted to hear—"Wheels up"—meaning Air Force One had safely departed our beautiful city!

•   •   •

While our marriage was far from soaring in 2002, it was certainly in much better shape than it had been when Lise had asked me to leave a few years earlier. Both of us were committed to making it work and, although there were still some fairly major ups and downs, their frequency and severity were beginning to diminish. We continued to be involved with Marriage Encounter as a presenting couple, and that gave us lots of opportunities not only to help others but also to work on our own issues. And we were still both seeing marriage counsellors, both as individuals and as a couple.

One of the issues I was struggling with was that it always seemed to be me who needed to change, say I was sorry or give some other kind of concession. I knew I needed to be careful here with my "King Baby I" attitude, but I believed that there were times when Lise also needed to change and that, although I was the one most in need of behaviour modification, there was a slice of the pie that belonged to her.

For example, remembering Covey's concept of the emotional bank account, I had, in my opinion, been making some pretty significant positive emotional deposits for the past few years. While far from perfect, I was no longer the monster I had once been. However, and again this was entirely from my perspective, when I did even the slightest thing wrong, Lise would still have a strong negative reaction, or be triggered, going from zero to sixty in seconds. I felt hurt and saddened by this, believing that a truly forgiving spouse could, and would, be less demanding and less judgemental.

I know that forgiveness, true forgiveness, is easy to talk about but extremely hard to bestow. I struggled then, as I still do now, with forgiving myself for the terrible things I had done. For Lise to struggle with forgiving me was also totally understandable. But that understanding and theoretical comprehension didn't make it any easier on me when she reacted so strongly to a new slight, no matter how small it might be.

I remember one couples session in particular where, at least for me, we had a breakthrough. The counsellor was someone I had been seeing alone for some time, and he suggested we meet with him as a couple. The issues of who was to blame and forgiveness came up, and I expressed my feelings and judgements (now able to understand the difference, thanks to Marriage Encounter). Lise immediately jumped in and became, in my opinion, defensive. The counsellor listened to both of us as we expressed our thoughts and viewpoints. Near the end of the session, he turned to Lise and said something to the effect of, "Lise, I believe Lance is correct in his observations. You might want to consider his position and come to the realization that you, too, need to make changes. Lance is not the only one who makes mistakes in this marriage."

I immediately started crying and felt relieved, as if a massive weight had been removed from my shoulders. I *wasn't* the only one making mistakes, and both of us needed to see that. I felt both vindicated and truly supported for the first time by anyone outside our relationship. Even after having spent the last five years going to AA, the Camillus Centre in Elliot Lake (twice, as I went a second time for their family program) and countless hours of counselling, this was the first time that anyone had seemed even remotely to be on my side. This may have been a very negative way to look at everything both Lise and I had done to get healthy, to get our marriage back on track. Still, it felt wonderful to feel affirmed in this way.

Lise saw how emotionally I was reacting and appeared to soften her stance, and her heart, to accept how I was experiencing things. While she was not a fan of this particular counsellor (his demeanour just rubbed her the wrong way), she was willing to concede that she, too, needed to work on how she responded when we had a fight or disagreement. She said that when I behaved negatively it was like all the good things I had worked on evaporated. She would immediately revert to becoming defensive and automatically adopt an attitude of "Hell no, I'm not putting up with this kind of shit anymore." She explained that early in our struggles it had been very important to put up emotional boundaries to protect herself but that she had, over time, lost the ability to perceive and calibrate those responses. In *Star Trek* terms, her "shields" went up to full power the instant she sensed any behaviour from me that remotely resembled what had gone on in the past.

The counsellor provided us with a powerful metaphor that Lise and I found very useful. He told us that our defensive mechanisms were like a light switch with a dimmer dial. When dealing with an argument, we were both ratcheting up the dial to full power the instant anything went wrong. He suggested that we visualize reaching out and turning the dial to the left, or down in power, when this happened. Don't turn the power completely off, he told us, just turn it down a few notches and allow ourselves to be vulnerable and accepting while still keeping enough power to the light switch to be able to see what was going on at that moment, not what we thought was happening based on years of past problems, slights and imperfections. Both of us found this mental imagery extremely valuable and still use it from time to time today.

·   ·   ·

Things at home were going well and all the boys were now in school, hockey and various other activities. Our youngest son, Mathieu (Mat), was very much like his mom and was totally into any sport that involved speed and danger. Lise is the mountain biker and downhill skier, while I prefer a slower, more sedate pace. Maybe it was all the tragedy I saw at work over the years, but I was constantly thinking about how to keep our little family safe.

As a duty inspector, I once attended three fatal accidents in one day, including one involving a mother and her daughter. While I wasn't the one having to get into the vehicles and deal directly with the deceased, my new role meant I regularly had to attend more of these kinds of incidents, and they certainly continued to add weight to the ever-growing mental stress I had to deal with, just as all first responders do. The post-traumatic stress–related chain I had been building over the years was becoming, unbeknownst to me, ever heavier.

One day Mat asked if we could go to the park around the corner, and so off we went, first to play catch and then to the swings. As I pushed him, he kept saying, "Higher, Daddy!" I pushed him higher and higher. We got to the point where I thought it was unsafe, as he was now going parallel with the ground. He was laughing and shouting, "Higher, Daddy, push me higher!" I told him it wasn't safe, but he begged me, so I pushed even higher, against my better judgement.

Then, to my massive surprise and horror, while at the peak of his forward motion, he jumped from the swing, did a back flip and landed on his feet. I was shocked and in disbelief at what I had just witnessed. I ran to him to be sure he was OK. He was smiling and laughing, apparently having loved the experience. I asked him what he was thinking, doing something as dangerous as that. He smiled and said simply, "It's OK, Daddy. Mommy and I do this all the time!"

•   •   •

Feeling "down" was an entirely normal state for me. The depths of those periods varied and so did their length, from a few hours to days and, in at least one case, weeks. I've said that I had considered suicide as a possible solution in the past. In the darkest moments of my recovery, these ideations would again sometimes drag me down into the abyss. For some reason, possibly self-preservation, my recollection of many of these times is severely limited. However, Lise's memory of them, and other troubling times, is quite amazing. During the writing of this book, I would ask her a question and she would recall minute details about certain events.

One of the counsellors we saw, the one who affirmed me in the joint session with Lise, explained to us that this was normal. He said that female brains are designed to operate freely between hemispheres, with more, and larger, interconnections between the two, whereas males tend to forget certain things faster. Things like arguments. I have never researched that premise, and maybe it was just a convenient way for a male counsellor to let men off the hook, but I do know that my memory for those difficult times is, for whatever reason, nowhere near as precise as Lise's.

Like the alarming episode that opened the book. It was around this period that Lise found me that dark day, sitting on the basement stairs of our home, in uniform, head down, staring at my service pistol. It was one of those times that suicidal thoughts were swirling around inside me, but all she knew was that I was non-responsive to her and just sat there. Lise was terrified, not for herself but for me. Fortunately, she was able to get me to listen to her, and I put the gun into my gun locker in the trunk of my police car.

In fact, Lise had to remind me of that incident while I was writing this book. I had pushed it from my mind, likely to protect myself. I don't even remember exactly when this was, but the only time I was ever home with my service pistol was when I was a duty inspector (we were on call 24/7 and had to be able to respond directly from home if needed, thus the gun locker and alarm in senior officers' vehicles).

Lise never told anyone about that incident, not even our boys. She probably should have called the station to speak to my boss. That would have set several official wheels in motion, including my being suspended until I received professional help, and of course the removal of all my use-of-force equipment. I know this because, as a duty inspector, I had to deal with these kinds of situations with other officers.

I suppose you could say that I was two-faced at those times, unwilling to reveal my issues and actions to anyone on the service so that I could hold onto my job, my career; yet fine with taking away another officer's use-of-force equipment and thus, in many ways, taking away their identity.

I don't know how to explain this to non-police readers. From the earliest stage of a police officer's career, the badge and gun become a major part of who we are. Policing is not just any career. You live it. You breathe it. Every building and every intersection you pass triggers memories of an incident on the job that took place there, even if it was twenty or thirty years ago. Everything you see, every day, for thirty-plus years is viewed through a policing lens. *What are those people doing hanging around that corner? Why does that car have a licence plate that's only held in place by one screw and hanging at a slightly off angle? Is it stolen?*

So, when an officer is suspended for any reason, a major part of their identity is lost. Ideally, they and their families get the help they need, and that cop is back to work with a full bill of health quickly. Sometimes, though, this is not possible. Sometimes they just can't find their way out of the darkness, tragically leading to them taking their own lives.

The bad news is that this happens far too often to police, members of the military and other first responders, right across Canada and around the world. The good news is that there are numerous resources available to help officers and their families, including Canada Beyond The Blue, Badge of Life Canada and Serenity Renewal for Families in Ottawa (see the Giving Back section at the end of the book for more information).

Sadly, that terrible day, sitting on the stairs staring at my gun, I wasn't thinking of the others like me and the help available to them, to us. I was too trapped in my own shit, alone in my despair. And, in a perverse way, with all the suicidal thoughts I had at various times through the years, the idea always came from my desire to make life better for my family. I truly believed that they would be better off without me and all my bullshit—permanently. To this day, I am grateful that Lise found me in time and talked me out of whatever dark place I was in. It was my lowest point. There was nowhere to go but up.

Chapter 14

From Valleys to Mountaintops

Over time, these horrible periods of darkness began to diminish, or at least to lose their severity. As our relationship healed and, slowly, began to flourish again, the massive up-and-down swings in my emotions seemed to even out somewhat.

Lise was doing extremely well at university and beginning to explore the possibility of enrolling in the Masters in Sports Psychology program at the University of Ottawa, something that I was fully supportive of. The boys were all doing well at school and, in their different ways, seemed happy and in a nice groove filled with academics, sports and friends.

Travel continued to be something Lise and I loved to do. And my ongoing involvement in the Canadian Association of Chiefs of Police (CACP) Information & Communications Technology (ICT) Committee ensured that at least once a year we had the opportunity to travel to various Canadian cities to attend either a meeting or conference (or both). While finances were still very tight, we were often able to travel "on the cheap" by driving to the event. I received a per diem that guaranteed a certain amount of money for food and incidentals every day, which we could make go further by always bringing a cooler filled with food from home. And Lise kept up her habit of exploring during the day to find inexpensive places for us to eat in the evening. It was amazing how well we could do even when having to be frugal.

Starting in 2003, when we attended the CACP ICT Conference in Montreal, it was the beginning of all sorts of wonderful trips for us to enjoy in the years to come. Where possible, and if the money was in the budget, we would either arrive a day or two early or stay a day or two after the event so that we could explore on our own.

Around this time, we were also fortunate enough to be invited to visit my brother and his family at a time-share they owned in Atlantic Beach, North Carolina. The place wasn't fancy, but it was quite nice and right on the beach. We brought the boys, and they loved their time there. Near the end of our week together, we learned that we could buy a week at this location for a one-time fee of around $1,500 US. This would give us annual access forever and we could even deed the week to one of our children when we passed away. We would have to pay an annual maintenance fee, but it was only about $500 US at the time. We could also join something called Interval International, a company that facilitated time-share switches between owners, meaning we could swap to stay at other locations across the United States and around the world. It sounded too good to be true, and you know what they say about that!

Like most people, we were pretty skeptical about the time-share craze that was happening in the United States. However, when they told us they would consider the money we had spent on our rent that week as a deposit, that was enough to get us to sign up. The rules, at least at the time, were that we had a one-week grace period within which we could cancel the purchase for any reason.

As soon as we got back to Ottawa, we called our lawyer who, as it happened, had some time-share units himself. He explained that they were not investments in the sense of providing a return and making money, but lifestyle investments that, used properly, could provide wonderful memories for decades to come. Based on his advice, and even though we didn't have an additional $1,000 US to spend, we decided to go ahead and complete the purchase.

Looking back, this, and the purchase of another two time-share weeks at the same resort over the years, was one of the best lifestyle decisions we ever made. We have switched many times to stay at beautiful time-shares, some of them major hotel brands, all over Canada and the United States, including Hawaii.

We were slowly beginning to climb out of the valley and upwards towards the mountaintops of our relationship.

•   •   •

Lise continued her educational journey by enrolling in the Master of Sports Psychology program at the University of Ottawa. We were all so proud of her and not at all surprised that she was excelling in academics. She has always been very athletic and loves to help people, so sports psychology was a perfect fit for her.

Lise's master's program was an amazing amount of work, and there were many mornings when she had to get up around 4:30 to complete all her readings and assignments. While most of her classmates had entered the program immediately after their undergrad degrees were completed, Lise had enrolled as a mature student with a family and working full-time for the Ottawa-Carleton District School Board as an educational assistant (often in some of the most challenging high schools in Ottawa). While all this added stress to our lives and more of a financial burden to our budget, it was certainly worth it. Lise's advanced education was beneficial both for her development and for the positives it brought our whole family, with her new-found ability to help us with things like visualization, goal-setting and distraction control.

•   •   •

In 2005, I was transferred back to the Central Patrol Division, returning full circle to my original roots in patrol. While I missed the freedom and action that I had as a duty inspector, this meant that I was back working straight day shifts and could be around to help out more at home. The day shift was also conducive to a much more consistent approach to exercise, with the gym right upstairs from my office and Rideau Canal right beside headquarters for regular runs, which I enjoyed. It was also a time when I could work more on my leadership skills, as I now had seven staff sergeants, about thirty sergeants and a couple hundred constables working in the division, situated in downtown Ottawa. Leading, and not just managing, such a diverse group of women and men was both demanding and rewarding.

Lise was heavily involved in her master's program, so when the police service announced another application process to select new superintendents, there was a great deal for us to discuss. In the end, though, it made more sense for me to continue supporting Lise's educational aspirations and to take a pass on the promotional process at that time. I was happy with that decision and believe that Lise appreciated the support, as she already had too much on her plate. However, another type of professional opportunity came along, anyway—as they do when you are open to seeing them.

I had always believed in being responsible for my own career development, constantly looking out for new opportunities and meeting new people who were, in some way, interesting or innovative. I would often approach people like that and ask if we could have a coffee, using the one-on-one as a networking and educational opportunity. Once, I remember meeting a very senior Government of Canada bureaucrat. He was an assistant deputy minister, therefore high up in the pecking order. I heard him speak at an event, and he was not at all like most bureaucrats, as he talked about challenging the status quo, innovation and getting things done. I had heard similar buzzwords come from other senior government officials before, but with him, for whatever reason, it sounded like he meant it.

I asked him if he would be willing to meet for coffee, saying I wanted to understand what drove him to be the way he was, especially while working inside a governmental apparatus that was essentially designed to create groupthink, not to develop innovative individuals. He was kind enough to agree, and the chat—which turned into several conversations and a mini-mentorship for me—opened my eyes to what can be accomplished when someone has vision, leadership skills and determination.

I had no idea at the time how this simple chat would help drive my future professional development, both in the police service and after I retired.

· · ·

I looked for developmental opportunities wherever I could find them, such as joining the International Association of Chiefs of Police (IACP) in 2006. I was still part of the CACP ICT, so it was natural to join the much larger international group. While I didn't have the funding to attend their conference, I began monitoring issues of importance and joined their Law Enforcement Information Management (LEIM) Section, a section I would later chair.

Interoperability had emerged as a key issue for both the IACP and CACP, flowing from the lack of communication and coordination between various groups of first responders in New York City on 9/11. Since then, there had been numerous commissions, studies and reports from around the world that provided clear evidence of the critical importance of getting the right information to the right people at the right time. Sharing information efficiently between jurisdictions, disciplines and levels of government is essential to the effectiveness of all public safety agencies, both in crisis situations and in day-to-day operations.

The challenges to true interoperability were many and complex. Some related to proprietary radio and software systems that were purposely built by industry with the unexpressed, or hidden, goal of not allowing agencies to talk to, or share information with, each other. While this seems counterintuitive (and counterproductive), the companies that produced these systems viewed it as a positive at the time, because their clients were locked in to their proprietary technology. This made it almost impossible for their clients to purchase systems or technology from other vendors, and equally impossible to share either voice or data among them.

A non-technical challenge to interoperability was organizational culture. For decades the various first-responder groups, typically police, fire and paramedics (please don't call them ambulance, as that is what they drive; they are paramedics) held fast to the belief that the information and radio systems they used were just for them. The notion of sharing radio channels in an emergency was heresy. The idea of all first responders being on the same channel and talking to each other had rarely been discussed and, when it was, it was shut down as unsafe, unpractical, insecure and downright crazy.

All of these issues, and many more that were specific to policing, were discussed during our CACP ICT meetings. As a possible solution, we began exploring the feasibility of a government program focused on public safety interoperability. One of the CACP ICT committee members was the executive director of the Canadian Police Research Centre, the same group that had led the research and development of the expert system that I had previously been involved in.

This research led to the CPRC-funded trip to Washington, DC, in October 1996 that I mentioned in Chapter 6, where we had the chance to meet various government and industry leaders who were involved in leading interoperability efforts in the United States. The report I drafted for the CPRC and CACP ICT Committee about that trip helped shape the future of interoperability in Canada while also, although I didn't know it at the time, creating the road map for the next major chapter of my career.

•   •   •

Lise and I continued to work on ourselves and our relationship, both as individuals and as a couple. Happily, the hard work—and make no mistake about it, a good marriage is hard work—was beginning to pay off, as we found ourselves in a much more respectful, patient and loving relationship.

I don't think either one of us ever fell out of love with the other; it was more like falling out of like. Lise, for very good reason, could no longer sit by and accept the behaviours that I had been displaying at the height of my sickness. When I was not well, I was full of anger, blame and resentment—with the focal point of that negativity being Lise. The more she set boundaries, as she had been taught in Al-Anon, the more resentful I had become. Now, with help from our counsellors, Al-Anon and AA, we were slowly moving towards a form of quiet interdependence, with both of us seeking positive results not just for ourselves but for each other as individuals and for our whole family.

Stephen Covey talks about how individuals work through his "7 Habits," or principles, starting with things like being proactive and beginning with the end in mind. Over time and with hard work, reflection, and in our case, professional help, you become independent. While that is good, it is not the desired end state according to Covey, and I totally agree. By focusing on higher-level goals, such as seeking first to understand and then to be understood, we were becoming "interdependent." In Covey's words, "Interdependent people combine their own efforts with the efforts of others to achieve their greatest success."[11]

While our greatest successes, other than our wonderful children, were yet to come, we were certainly on the right path.

•   •   •

In 2007, after a great deal of planning and discussion by the CACP ICT Committee, the CACP Board of Directors and internally at the Ottawa Police Service, I accepted a secondment to the Canadian Police Research Centre (CPRC was later amalgamated into the Centre for Security Sciences, inside Defence Research and Development Canada), part of the Government of Canada. My role was designed to lead both national and international efforts to improve public safety interoperability, or the ability to get the right information to the right people at the right time.

---

11. Stephen R. Covey, *The 7 Habits of Highly Effective People: Powerful Lessons in Personal Change*

It was an exciting time because there was no road map to follow and, with an extremely supportive boss, it was just a matter of time before our successes started to mount. Over the next three years, I travelled across Canada, the United States and internationally doing research, creating networks of like-minded subject matter experts and developing something called the Canadian Interoperability Technology Interest Group (CITIG).

One of the greatest lessons I learned during this time was the importance of good governance and solid policy development. I had the chance to see all sorts of great technology in use worldwide, but where most systems failed, especially in critical incidents, was at the governance and policy levels. Figuring out who is in charge and who does what is easy when things are going well. But that becomes extremely complex when everything is going "south" (poorly) and the blame game begins, like on 9/11, during a mass shooting or in the middle of a massive wildfire with winds over 100 kilometres per hour pushing the edge of disaster.

I attended my first IACP conference in San Diego in 2008. I've attended almost every one of them since then, other than in 2020 when it was cancelled due to COVID. This allowed me also to get more heavily involved in the IACP Law Enforcement Information Management (LEIM) Section, the largest of three technology-focused groups inside the IACP. I was elected to the LEIM Board and became Chair in 2010, only the second Canadian to do so.

In 2008, shortly after being seconded from the Ottawa Police Service to the Canadian Police Research Centre, I was asked to plan a national-level workshop that would bring stakeholders together for the first time. We had less than two months to plan what later became known as CITIG 1, but it was a huge success, selling out both delegate and exhibit space.

We decided early on that this needed to be a "workshop" and not a conference, as we wanted to come out of the event with a clear road map that would deliver actual outcomes, not just outputs like reports. The number one recommendation from the almost two hundred delegates was that Canada needed a national plan for communications interoperability. So, immediately after CITIG 1, I started planning a five-day workshop in Ottawa and invited approximately thirty of Canada's leading experts to attend.

These experts truly were the grandparents of communications interoperability in Canada. After five days of facilitated conversations and intense collaboration, we had the first draft of what was then known as the Canadian Communications Interoperability Plan, later approved by all federal, provincial and territorial ministers as the Communications Interoperability Strategy for Canada.[12]

One of my post-retirement goals is to do what I can, via writing and behind-the-scenes facilitation, to continue supporting important interoperability issues like Next Generation 9-1-1, emergency alerting and the Public Safety Broadband Network. (I feel another book might well be in the making here!) Having said that, our creation of the Communications Interoperability Strategy for Canada continues to be one of my proudest achievements, and the friendships developed during that time, across Canada and around the world, continue today.

•   •   •

In 2009, Lise and I were able to make our first trip to beautiful Australia. I was going on a research trip to New South Wales, Queensland and Victoria to study various interoperability efforts and

---

12. Public Safety Canada, Canadian Communications Interoperability Strategy, 2011, Cat. No.: PS4-109/2011E, ISBN: 978-1-100-17577-5

programs. While we were a bit concerned about leaving our three boys (now aged twenty-one, nineteen and seventeen) alone for a couple weeks, we were both excited about what this trip, and future travel, would mean for our relationship.

Like all my business trips, the daytime agenda was packed. I had the chance to meet some of Australia's leading public safety, government and academic leaders, shortly after they had all been through a very stressful crisis situation.

We were visiting in February, during their summer, and it was excessively hot, especially in Victoria. It was well over 40°C and even breathing outside was difficult. Unfortunately, this extreme heat had led to numerous bushfires, including what became known as "Black Saturday."[13] This series of intense wildfires—feeding off heat, high winds and the abundance of eucalyptus trees (filled with oil)—moved at great speed and resulted in 173 deaths and over $4 billion in damage. While this was a massive tragedy for the State of Victoria, and Australia as a nation, it also provided a great deal of information relevant to my interoperability research.

I met with numerous leaders from Victoria's Country Fire Authority and various government departments, including the Victoria Police and Ambulance Victoria (they had/have not yet switched over to the practice of calling themselves a paramedic service), almost all of whom knew someone who had perished in the fires. This required being extremely sensitive in my questioning, and I was unable to push too hard.

Nonetheless, the results of that research helped shape our efforts back in Canada on issues like public alerting, mobile broadband and Next Generation 9-1-1 (Next Generation 000 in Australia). It was

---

13. en.wikipedia.org/wiki/Black_Saturday_bushfires

critical for us to find ways to improve interoperability before we experienced something as devastating as our own version of Black Saturday.

• • •

Although the trip was primarily business-related, Lise and I found time to explore and enjoy the immense beauty and wonderful people of Australia. Friends took us for a beautiful drive up the Great Ocean Road in Victoria. We toured all the major locations in Sydney, including the Botanical Gardens, where we saw hundreds (thousands?) of massive fruit bats screeching as they hung upside down, and the iconic Opera House. We even got to spend time on Queensland's fantastic Gold Coast with its beautiful beaches and the warmest water we've ever swum in.

Ever since we first became friends, Lise and I had dreamed of travelling the world together. We had talked for countless hours about the countries we both wanted to visit and what we would do there. Well, we were no longer just talking about it, we were doing it!

We arrived back in Ottawa, with the house still intact and the boys happy to see us, even more in love than we had ever been before, and even more committed to travelling together whenever and wherever possible. Those journeys were about to become more frequent and even easier than we had imagined.

• • •

As 2009 continued, I needed to plan for my return to the Ottawa Police Service, as my two-year leave of absence would be over at the end of the year. I arranged to meet with the new chief to talk about his plans for me upon my return. He told me that I would be going back to the duty inspector's office. Although this was a role I loved, I had been hoping to do something new. I could tell from his demeanour that he wasn't keen on my returning to the service at all, so I asked him if he thought it was time for me to retire. His answer was a simple "Yes."

Now, some people, after thirty-three years of service to their community, might feel hurt or disappointed at this response. But I, having learned so many lessons flowing from my addiction and, thankfully, my recovery, took his bluntness as a positive and the chance to move on in other directions. As the old saying goes, whenever one door closes, another opens, and I immediately saw a door opening for me.

I thanked the chief for his openness and told him that I would be retiring at the end of the year. He then advised me that I had been nominated for the Order of Merit of the Police Forces (I later learned the nomination came from a chief of police in Western Canada, not the Ottawa Police) and would be invested as an Officer of the Order the following May. That was a huge honour, a great surprise, and an extremely positive piece of news to share with Lise and the boys when I went home that night!

My last shift with the Ottawa Police Service was on December 31, 2009. I asked one of the duty inspectors if I could go out with him for the evening. Around 11 p.m. he dropped me off at the corner of Rideau and King Edward, the same beat I began my career on in 1977. Over the next hour, I slowly walked down Rideau towards Sussex, reminiscing about various things that had occurred over the past three decades, and even chatting with some of our sons' friends who were out celebrating New Year's Eve.

As the clock hit midnight, I climbed back into the passenger seat of the duty inspector's van, my shift complete. (I'm pretty sure he never lost sight of me, wanting to be sure the old guy didn't get into any trouble on his last shift.) I went back to the station, changed into my civilian clothes and walked out the door the same way I had walked into the original headquarters in 1977: alone. But this time felt very different from the sense of loss I experienced when I left policing behind temporarily to work at InvestigAide. That experience, coupled with my time on secondment to the Government of Canada, had prepared me for life beyond policing.

I was now ready to move on and looked forward to new challenges and opportunities. I was excited about what was to come next.

•   •   •

I had been planning our twenty-fifth anniversary trip for two years: two months of first-class travel including New Zealand, Australia, an eighteen-day cruise across the South Pacific and then a month on four different Hawaiian Islands. What I didn't know when I first started planning was that it would also be my retirement trip.

On March 27, 2010, Lise and I flew business class from Ottawa to Toronto and then on to Sydney, Australia. After a short layover, we continued, again in business class, to Auckland, New Zealand, via Air New Zealand (who have some of the nicest business-class lounges I've ever visited). Almost all of the trip was being paid for by points. Between our airline, hotel and credit card points, our entire two-month, top-of-the-line trip ended up costing only around $15,000. Now, that's still a lot of money, but we were finally in a better place financially. And, once again, Lise and I decided that our relationship was worth it and that we would rather spend the money on each other now than wait till we were much older and had saved more but might not be able to travel due to health (we had no idea it would be something called COVID-19 that would limit our retirement travel).

While I planned all the logistics for the trip—things like flights, transfers and hotels—Lise did most of the itinerary planning—and did she ever do a fantastic job! We started with a picturesque train ride from Auckland to the Tongariro National Park stop and then on to the beautiful Chateau Tongariro near Mount Ruapehu, in the middle of New Zealand's North Island.

The following day, we hiked (or tramped, as they say in New Zealand) the famous and challenging nineteen-kilometre Tongariro Alpine Crossing, a World Heritage Site that is listed as one of the top ten single-day hikes in the world. It was certainly a difficult hike, and breathtaking in other ways too, as we crossed from one side of the mountain to the other, passing volcanic soda springs from time to time. The area is so majestic that it was used as the location for the *Lord of the Rings* movies, with Mordor being located around the rocky slopes of Tongariro National Park.

The trip continued with another unbelievable train ride, this time to Wellington, New Zealand's capital city. After a spectacular crossing of the famous (and dangerous) Cook Strait via ferry, we continued by train to Christchurch. The city was wonderful and still untouched by the tragic earthquake that would take 185 lives the following February. Our stay was short, as we were up early the next day to take yet another train ride, this time to the halfway point across the South Island, a spot called Arthur's Pass, where we got on our rented road bikes with panniers packed and ready for, we thought, a leisurely three-day cycle back to Christchurch.

We (meaning I) vastly overestimated our fitness level and underestimated the level of difficulty of the day-one eighty-two-kilometre trip. We (meaning I) also failed to take into account the almost gale-force winds and rain that drove right into our faces, slowing down the bikes even when going downhill. Needless to say, this first leg of the cycling trip was far less fun than I had imagined. (We even named it "Whose idea was this, anyway?" on our travel blog, which the boys and other family back home were monitoring.) With help from a kind motorist who saw us struggling in the near-dark, we made it to Springfield, changed into warm, dry clothes, ate and crashed for the night.

The remaining segments of the cross-country bike trip were much less arduous but equally breathtaking, and we finally arrived back in Christchurch for a well-deserved rest. The following day, Lise went on her own mountain bike tour as, in addition to celebrating our anniversary, she was also using the trip to scout for locations and service providers for a future women's adventure tour she was planning. I used that day to meet New Zealand Police leaders, also with a view to returning to this amazing place, our second-favourite country in the world (after Canada, of course). That dream would later come true; Lise and I have now visited New Zealand many times for both business and pleasure.

On April 10, we flew to Sydney to enjoy everything it had to offer for a couple days before departing on a luxurious cruise across the South Pacific. While the entire cruise was over-the-top, the ports of Bora Bora, Raiatea and Moorea in the French Polynesian islands provided memories we will always cherish. Crossing the International Date Line was also quite fun, but sea-faring folk are sworn to secrecy about what exactly takes place when you sail over the line. If you want to know, you will have to take your own cruise, or join the navy!

Our month in Hawaii, again staying at spectacular hotels and time-shares, mostly on points, was out of this world. We liked Waikiki Beach and found the Pearl Harbor Memorial very powerful, but our favourite islands were Maui and Kauai. Both were remarkably beautiful and made for such a memorable anniversary trip. The highlight of the entire trip was the emotional, and surprisingly spiritual, sunrise tour at Haleakalā National Park. Numerous friends had told us that this was something we needed to do, and they were right.

We had to wake up at a crazy hour to be ready for the minibus that drove us up to the summit in time for the sun to rise. It was freezing cold, as we had been warned it would be, and Lise and I hugged each other while we and hundreds of other visitors quietly waited. We were not disappointed as the sun slowly rose in the east and touched us in ways that we never could have imagined. I took dozens of photos that morning (including the one that's on the cover of this book, not knowing at the time that the photo would someday be used in that way), trying to capture the splendour and the magic of the moment. And when our time on the summit was over, the cycle trip down the mountain was also beautiful, as well as a lot of fun—by far the easiest cycle we've ever done, not having to pedal the bikes for almost the entire two-hour trip.

But our trip up Haleakalā and back down wasn't just another tourist excursion or stunning natural sight to see. It is said that Mark Twain, when he saw his first Haleakalā sunrise, called it "The sublimest spectacle I ever witnessed."

I think the best way to describe that sunrise is "spiritual." I felt like I was in the presence of God, and felt thankful for his blessings. *Thank you, Lord, for everything you have done for me, for us. I look back over the years and am reminded that it was your love, along with the love of your beautiful child, Lise, that sustained me. In my darkest hours you were there—once I opened my heart to you.*

The majesty and breathtaking beauty of the sunrise was as undeniable as it was symbolic for us. Over the course of our twenty-five-year marriage, we had traversed too many valleys of despair, hurt, anger and abuse to count. Now, here we were, deeply in love, holding each other at one of the most beautiful locations in the world, witnessing the birth of another day. We were also witnessing the rebirth, as it were, of our marriage, now full of love, respect and a deep, abiding knowledge that we had made it to the peak of our relationship.

Chapter 15
What's Next?

After being away together for almost two months to celebrate our milestone anniversary and my retirement, Lise and I were a teeny bit disappointed to have to cut such a fabulous trip short by a few days. But there could not have been a much better reason for having to come home early than attending my investiture as an Officer of the Order of Merit of the Police Forces.

There are only a small number of sworn and civilian police members admitted to this prestigious circle each year, most at the level of "Member," a handful at the "Officer" level and typically only one or two at the highest level of "Commander," normally reserved for people like the Commissioner of the Ontario Provincial Police. Regardless of the level at which you are invested, it is a huge honour. The website of the Governor General of Canada describes it this way:

Established in October 2000, the Order of Merit of the Police Forces honours the leadership and exceptional service or distinctive merit displayed by the men and women of the Canadian Police Services, and recognizes their commitment to this country. The primary focus is on exceptional merit, contributions to policing and community development.

Her Majesty Queen Elizabeth II is the Order's Sovereign [she was
at the time of my investiture], the governor general is its Chancellor
and a Commander, and the commissioner of the Royal Canadian
Mounted Police is its Principal Commander.[14]

The ceremony, held on May 26, 2010, was very special and took place at Rideau Hall, the Governor General's residence in the New Edinburgh area of Ottawa. We were able to call in some favours and get permission for our entire family to attend. It was a beautiful day and everything went like clockwork, including the lovely reception hosted by then Governor General of Canada, Michaëlle Jean, for all those invested, their families and other guests. She was very warm and welcoming and took time to chat with everyone who attended.

I am extremely proud of this recognition and of the photo we took with Michaëlle Jean, which was my computer's background image for years. We were the only family to get this kind of photo with the Governor General, and that was only because our middle son, Dominic, took it upon himself to arrange it. The ceremony and reception were over, and we were wandering around Rideau Hall when we saw her with her entourage and security detail, all serving RCMP officers (a couple of whom knew me from past security events).

Protocol for these security details is that once the principal, in this case the Governor General, starts moving, there should be no interruption and certainly no one should be allowed to impede their movement. Well, although I knew this, Dominic did not, so he walked right up to them, forcing them to stop, and asked Michaëlle Jean if we could get a photo with her. The security team all stared at me, thinking, I suppose, that I had put him up to it. But the Governor

---

14. www.gg.ca/en/honours/canadian-honours/directory-honours/order-merit-police-forces

General graciously gave a beautiful smile and said, "Of course." One of her staff members took the photo, which I will cherish forever.

• • •

Before my retirement from the force, Lise and I had set up our own company with the help of our lawyer and accountant so that we would be prepared for any contracts that came our way post-retirement. Fortunately, the wait wasn't long, as the work required to create CITIG was only the beginning, and I went right back to work full-time on January 10, 2010 (with a break in April and May for our anniversary trip), on contract to the Government of Canada as "Advanced Special Advisor, Communications Interoperability" to the Centre for Security Science, part of Defence Research and Development Canada (DRDC).

We accomplished a great deal over the next two years, working with various subject matter experts from across Canada and around the world. While governmental bureaucracy would sometimes slow things down, my boss in the government was fantastic and always did his best to deal with all that, while the rest of us worked towards our goal of improving public safety interoperability.

Although the work was extremely rewarding and I was compensated very well, it was clear that for CITIG to be truly effective, we needed to transition to an entirely different governance model. As a result, I did not renew my contract with DRDC at the end of 2011. Instead, I accepted a contract to develop a business case for transitioning CITIG from a project inside the Government of Canada to an independent entity that could operate successfully and be financially sustainable.

I presented the business case to the Canadian Association of Chiefs of Police, the Canadian Association of Fire Chiefs and the Paramedic Chiefs of Canada for their approval, which we received around April 2012. We turned CITIG into a Canadian registered not-for-profit, with CACP, CAFC and PCC all having voting membership. I was named as CITIG's first executive director and, after a $10,000 initial investment from each of the three parent associations, we became self-sustaining by the end of our first year.

•   •   •

So far, I hadn't had any reoccurrence of my skin cancer, and my gout was pretty much under control, but another physical problem emerged during this period. This one was a direct result of my years in policing, specifically the loud noises we all deal with, such as at the gun range. I began having a constant ringing in my right ear that just would not go away. It started slowly, over a period of months, then became extremely distracting, sometimes to the point that I couldn't focus on anything else.

A visit to our family doctor confirmed that I had tinnitus, a medical condition that causes a constant ringing and is very common in many first responders. In my case, it's more like a high-pitched squealing in one or both ears. This is a sound that only I can hear, not something from an external source. There are mediation strategies I can use to attempt to mask the noise, including having quiet music or a television playing in the background; but according to the medical professionals I have met with, there is nothing that can be done in my case to stop the ringing. Unfortunately, this annoying and intrusive sound can become extremely distracting, to the point of making it hard to concentrate—especially once you start to focus on it.

For example, as I am writing this section of the book, the ringing, which I wasn't even aware of a few minutes ago, is now blaring in my right ear. The more I think about it, the louder and more disturbing it becomes. To help me focus, I play soft Gregorian chanting music in my headphones while I write. This ringing will never go away, it's just something else that I need to deal with on a daily basis. So, the best solution for right now is to stop writing about it!

•   •   •

As satisfying as my new consulting career was to me, the more I worked post-retirement, the more my resentments started to grow. *Will I ever get to retire? Why am I continuing to work so hard? Is this some hidden childhood psychological problem that's driving me to seek self-worth from external sources instead of being intrinsically motivated?* The answer to that last question was yes, and was, in some part, the genesis for this book. It was a bit unsettling that I couldn't seem to stop working and simply enjoy my retirement; nor could I fully embrace the continuation of my working life.

Then, along came a wonderful Canadian book, *Victory Lap Retirement*,[15] by Mike Drak, Rob Morrison and Jonathan Chevreau, and it was truly a game-changer. Reading the book was life-altering for me because it helped me shift from thinking that retirement was something I needed to attain to understanding that it is an ongoing series of transitions, a number of self-driven and self-selected phases in my life beyond the police service. I, with lots of input from Lise, could choose what to do next, who I could do it with and whether I wanted to get paid while doing whatever it was that I wanted. Cool!

•   •   •

At this new stage of my life and career, I had guaranteed income from my pension, so earning money was no longer a primary motivator;

---

15. Mike Drak, Rob Morrison and Jonathan Chevreau, *Victory Lap Retirement, Second Edition*, Milner & Associates Inc.

and I didn't have to do whatever someone else dictated. I was free to pick and choose work that was interesting, challenging and fulfilling, and to take on as much—or as little—as I cared to. I would always discuss the various opportunities with Lise for her input, but ultimately, I was now my own "boss."

To help me decide what types of contracts I wanted to accept, I developed my own "core values statement." Much like having an investment strategy to help decide what kinds of financial decisions you want to make, this values statement was designed to help me process new opportunities. By following it, I'm able to take the emotion out of the equation (they're going to pay me *how* much?) and make value-based decisions. Every new opportunity—and there are far more out there than most retiring public safety leaders think—is mapped against this core values statement.

My core values are as follows, in order of priority, and each must be met in order to move to the next value gate:

- Integrity
- Honesty (you can have honesty without integrity, but you cannot have integrity without honesty)
- Making a difference and helping others
- Having fun and working on projects I enjoy
- Working with people I like and respect

Once those are in place: Getting paid what I am worth. Although this is the lowest priority, it's still a measurement of perceived value. If the first core values aren't met, then this one doesn't matter at this stage of my life. However, if the first three *are* met, then this is part of how I (and most people) gauge success.

I've accepted many new opportunities over and above paying contracts in my field of expertise, including coaching and mentoring various people and helping others make the transition to their own "victory laps," sometimes on a pro bono basis or, in many cases, for the price of a cup of coffee. In fact, I've started writing my second book on this topic, with the working title *What's Next: A Guide to Value-Based Decisions*.

The cool thing about victory lap retirement is that this is my choice, our choice. It's no longer a decision made by a "boss," but something I do because I want to. I've also turned down many offers over the past ten years, because either I was just too busy or the opportunity didn't pass the core-values test. This decision-making process has been immensely helpful for me, and I highly recommend that readers develop their own values statement, especially for your first victory lap, when saying "No" is often hardest.

•   •   •

In March 2014, after providing the CITIG board with one year's notice, I left my role as their executive director and turned the page on a new victory lap. This decision was made for multiple reasons, including the realization that, although I loved helping make Canada safer, the pay sucked.

Although we were doing much better financially and no longer had to wonder if we could pay for our groceries as we went through the checkout, we were nowhere near as financially strong as we felt we needed to be in order to achieve many of our long-term goals, like buying a cottage or travelling the globe. The decision to leave CITIG was never about getting rich but about having a solid financial foundation that would set us up nicely for the future. To make that happen, I needed to convert my knowledge, skills and abilities into business opportunities that would help us achieve our objectives.

Fortunately, there were tons of extremely cool opportunities all over the world that also involved making a difference and working with people I truly liked. Some paid better than others, while some just covered the cost of travel, which also allowed Lise and I to visit new and exciting locales, including in New Zealand and Australia (multiple times), Europe and, of course, Canada and the United States. During this period, I travelled extensively for business, often with Lise if she was interested and available, working and collaborating with some of the smartest, nicest and most dedicated people I'd ever met. As a result, I now have more airline miles and hotel points than you can imagine, even free breakfasts for life at one hotel chain—something that every retiree aspires to!

• • •

Our next victory lap saw Lise and I spending our winters in beautiful Sedona, Arizona. While I was no longer CITIG's executive director, I was very much committed to the organization's ongoing success. So, with that in mind, in January 2015 I reached out to a major private-sector industry partner to see if they might be willing to sponsor CITIG.

I made the pitch to one of their vice-presidents at their beautiful headquarters in Scottsdale, and he quickly agreed, but had a question for me as well. Would I be willing to help them enter the Canadian market in a major capacity? They were looking to expand their international footprint and thought that Canada would be a great first step.

This decision was much harder than previous offers for me. Not because they didn't map to my core values, as they very much did, but because this was an offer from the private sector. Although I had previously worked in the private sector during my leave of absence from the Ottawa Police, that was more of a professional development opportunity. I accepted that role with the full knowledge that I would be returning to policing after the two-year learning experience ended.

Accepting this offer would mean going to work for the "dark side," as so many public safety leaders viewed their industry partners (and to a much lesser extent, still view them). If I accepted, I would be closing the door on many other potential opportunities, at least for the period I worked for this company, due to either a real or perceived conflict of interest.

In making this decision, I had lots of long talks with Lise, and I reached out to a handful of Canadian police leaders whom I knew I could trust to be 100 percent truthful with me. Every one of them said essentially the same things:

1. If I accepted this private-sector role and then reached out to them in the future asking for a call or meeting about issues like interoperability or community safety, they would happily continue to work with me.
2. If I called wanting to talk about products and services that the company sold, they may or may not accept the call/meeting—and I would need to be OK with this kind of rejection.
3. If I ever called asking for a meeting for the first purpose above and switched gears to the second partway through, then our relationship would take a massive negative hit. Pulling this kind of bait-and-switch on these respected leaders in the middle of a conversation would be a huge faux pas, likely leading to them not taking future calls from me.

After much soul-searching and a final chat with Lise, I signed my first consulting contract with the company in mid-March 2015. That decision led to my providing them with strategic advice and support for the following five years. I learned an amazing amount from this company and its outstanding Canadian leader as well as other key team members. These people exhibited Covey's fifth habit, "Seek first to understand, then to be understood."

In my experience, salespeople often listen with the intent to sell. Of course, selling products and services is clearly the overarching goal of a for-profit company, but I witnessed this team truly listening to understand what problems the police service was attempting to solve. Only once everyone had a solid understanding of the agency's needs did the discussion move to how they might be able to help. It was amazing to see this process unfold over and over again across the country!

My five-year involvement with this company was a great "victory lap." In many ways, it set Lise and me up financially for a fantastic future, including allowing us to purchase our dream home on a beautiful lake near Mont Tremblant, Quebec. However, when the sun began setting on this particular lap, it was time once again to climb to the top of our symbolic "tallest tree" and ask ourselves if we were still in the right jungle.

•   •   •

While everything work-related was going extremely well, I couldn't say the same for my physical health, which, unfortunately, ended up impacting my mental health in a way that I could never have predicted.

In July 2017, I had an all-day meeting scheduled with someone from the company I was working with. As the meeting progressed, I noticed that I couldn't see the lower parts of his body out of my left eye. It was weird because when both eyes were open, he looked normal, but when I shut my right eye, I couldn't see below his waist with just my left eye. I have no idea what caused me to start looking out of one eye, but it was starting to concern me. By early afternoon, I could see only his face and the top of his chest, and I mentioned it to him. Neither of us had any idea what was happening to me.

Later that afternoon, I had to drive our son Mat to his physiotherapist to deal with a leg injury. As I waited for him, the vision in my left eye continued to diminish. I told Mat about it when he came back to the car and, thankfully, he pushed me to see someone right away. We found an optometry clinic that was open nearby, and the technician who examined me said, "You have a detached retina. This is a medical emergency, you need to have surgery tonight. Wait right here and we will call the Ottawa Eye Institute to get the process started." *Wow!*

About an hour later, I was in the emergency room and the doctor told me that he would be sticking a needle in my eye in order to remove some vitreous, the gel-like fluid in our eyes. Once that was done, he said he would be sticking another needle into my eye in order to insert a small amount of gas that would help reattach the retina. He also told me that it was very good that I had come in quickly, otherwise I would likely have lost the vision in my left eye forever (thanks, Mat).

The procedure took only a few minutes and was followed by the bad news. Because of the location of the retinal detachment, I would need to keep my head severely tilted to the right for fifty minutes of every hour, twenty-four hours a day, for the next two weeks. This angling of my head would allow the gas bubble to push the retina back into place. The doctor said I was lucky because sometimes, depending on where the detachment was, people had to keep their head down, often using a massage table with a hole for their face and a mirror on the ground to see anything, for the same two-week period. The doctor also stressed that I must never fall asleep on my back. If that happened for any extended period, the gas bubble would move to the front of my eye and could cause irreparable damage.

Needless to say, the next two weeks were not fun, but Lise and the boys did everything they could to help keep me comfortable. It was especially challenging at night, as I needed to be propped up to sleep in the correct position and had pillows against my back to ensure I could not turn onto it. I woke up numerous times every night, afraid that I might have moved to my back, which I actually did do a few times, luckily with no damage being done.

Now, you might already have noticed that I can be a bit hard-headed at times. Well, despite my detached retina, I was stubbornly adamant that I wasn't going to miss the Canadian Association of Chiefs of Police conference, which I attended every year, this time in Montreal. Both Lise and my boss at the private-sector company thought I was crazy, but I took the train from Ottawa to Montreal a week later, head still firmly tilted to the right for fifty minutes of every hour. Of course, I looked ridiculous, but I felt it was important to attend the conference, as I had committed to it when signing my contract. I ended up having a number of great conversations while there, including one with a good friend, a chief of police who was struggling with the idea of retirement. In the end, I cut the trip short and, finally listening to everyone's advice, returned home to rest.

Over the next couple of months, I had to see the surgeon several times and, once the retina had been pushed back into the correct location, thanks to the gas bubble that was slowly dissipating, he used a laser to firmly reattach the retina. He also repaired multiple tears in the retina, explaining that they had allowed the vitreous to get in behind my retina and push it away from the back of my eye. While he wasn't the most pleasant doctor I had ever dealt with, he certainly knew his stuff and was confident that the eye would be fine, albeit with many more "floaters" than I'd had before the detachment.

Everything was great for a few months and then, in February 2018, I was having dinner at the cottage with Lise and our oldest son,

Jonny. I was sitting at the head of the table when I noticed I couldn't see Jonny when relying on the peripheral vision in my right eye. After opening and closing my left eye to verify that what I thought was happening was indeed happening, I told them that I had a detached retina in my right eye and had to get to the emergency room right away. Sure enough, after a short wait, I was back at the Ottawa Eye Institute getting needles stuck into my *right* eye. This time, I had to keep my head severely tilted to the *left* for fifty minutes every hour, twenty-four hours a day, for the next couple of weeks.

There was yet another CACP event taking place that month, this time the Information & Communications Technology conference. I had led the planning for that event many times and had attended every one of them going back to Cornwall in 2000. I was adamant that I would be attending again, come hell or high water. The only problem was that the conference was in Vancouver. Flying was out of the question with the gas bubble in my eye. If I flew, it would likely explode due to the air pressure variance, causing excruciating pain and permanent blindness in the affected eye. So flying was a hard no! At my next appointment with the eye surgeon, I told him that I wanted to take the train to a professional event, asking if that would pose any medical risks. He said that would be fine, then after a short pause added, "As long as the train does not go over any mountains." Clearly, I was not going to the conference.

While everything went as planned with the repair to my eye, I had no idea that one of the biggest mental health challenges of my life was right around the corner.

• • •

The day started out normal, with me lying on my left side, keeping the gas bubble in my right eye in the correct position as I watched TV in the basement of our home in Rockland. The house was quiet, as Lise had taken the car into the city. My mind started to wander as I lay there and, slowly, the ringing in my right ear, a symptom of my existing tinnitus, became louder and louder. Even with the TV on, I was fixated on the sound inside my head and it was hard to concentrate on anything else.

That morning was a "perfect storm" of adverse conditions: a detached retina, the incessant ringing in my ear, being alone in the house, feeling afraid for the future due to all these medical issues, and an entirely new sensation that began building in my mind and chest—an immense feeling of anxiousness, of being overwhelmed.

It's hard to describe the feeling, but my mind began racing and I was short of breath. I wondered if I was having a heart attack and thought that maybe I should call 9-1-1 to have paramedics come to check me out. Those thoughts only served to increase my anxiety, and I could no longer lie down. I *had* to get up and walk around. I started pacing back and forth, back and forth, back and forth, my head tilted to the side, thinking that I was going crazy.

My mind was now racing out of control, even to the point of having wildly irrational thoughts. *If the cops show up to take me for a mental health evaluation, I'll fucking fight them. No fucking way anyone is going to put me into a straitjacket. I'm not going fucking anywhere! Fuck that!*

I must have paced ten thousand steps in our living room, back and forth, back and forth. I had no idea what was happening, and I couldn't control it. Somewhere in the depths of my mind, I knew I should be calling for help, but the thought of being "apprehended" under the Mental Health Act was terrifying. I had faced years of stress as a police officer—car chases, fights, overseeing more major events than I could count, even being responsible for a presidential visit—never having any level of anxiety other than the normal stress that comes with managing those kinds of events. *What is happening to me? Am I going crazy?*

Eventually I called our son Mat, in part because he lived closest to us and in part because I knew he had experience with friends who suffered from anxiety, which would sometimes lead to more severe panic attacks, something I now realized I was likely experiencing. Mat was great and came right away to the house, talking to me and helping me to stop pacing and encouraging me to breathe deeply. Thankfully, the panic attack subsided, and he helped me get settled again downstairs on the couch, head again tilted to the left. He stayed with me until Lise got home and everything returned to normal.

Well, normal for me. Alcoholism. Depression. Cancer. Gout. Detached retinas. Tinnitus. Now a panic attack. What else could go wrong, I wondered.

• • •

Diverticulitis was what else could go wrong.

I woke up in the middle of the night in January 2019 with severe pain in my lower-left abdomen. It was like nothing I had ever felt before, and I was pretty sure it wasn't a normal stomachache. I was at the cottage, where we were now living pretty much full-time. It was very early on a Saturday morning, so I thought, to heck with it, I'm going to emergency at the hospital. I figured that it would be quiet there and I could get seen fairly quickly.

Eight hours later, after a battery of blood tests and a CT scan, I was told that I had diverticulitis, a pretty common disease of the digestive tract in adults over the age of sixty. Over time, small, bulging pouches known as diverticula can form in the lining of your digestive system; when they get inflamed or infected, you have diverticulitis. The treatment can range from having to follow an extremely modified diet (with only clear liquids for a few days then slowly starting to eat certain easily digestible foods), taking antibiotics or, in severe cases, having surgery. The doctor put me on a combination of a modified diet and antibiotics, which resolved the issue over the next few days. I've had only a few mild attacks since then, so far needing to modify my diet only when I feel an attack coming on.

•   •   •

After the panic attack the previous year, all I wanted was a prescription for some kind of wonder drug that would calm me if I experienced another episode like that. I made arrangements to see a psychologist, and he was a huge help. Psychologists are unable to prescribe medication; instead, he taught me a number of calming techniques to deal with any future reoccurrences.

He recommended that I stay away from any prescription-based resolutions altogether, partly due to his aversion to using drugs as a first step and, even more importantly, due to my history with addictions. This made perfect sense to me. I had heard numerous stories from addicts over the years who had replaced one addiction (alcohol or recreational drugs, for example) with another one, often in the form of prescription drugs or their street equivalents.

I recognize that many people simply cannot manage various forms of mental health–related issues without medicinal supports. And far be it from me to judge anyone else who is suffering. Everyone needs to follow their own path and the advice of their support teams, including their family doctor, psychologist, psychiatrist, counsellors, spirit guides and anyone else who is there to help.

In my case, my psychologist was wonderful to deal with, listened with care and compassion (as have most of my counsellors over the years) and was immensely helpful. I've had a number of mild anxiety attacks since then, but so far, I've been able to use the tools and techniques he taught me to keep myself from going into a full-blown panic attack, just as I have learned to handle my emotions when I start to feel a depression coming on.

With all my mental health–related issues, I know that I need to live my life one day at a time and be ready to deal with whatever challenges come my way, accepting support from Lise, my family, our friends and various counsellors, all of whom I'm thankful for.

• • •

Back then I rarely spoke to anyone other than my family, close friends or medical professionals about my physical and mental health challenges, just as with the other addiction and wellness issues I've faced over the years. I still felt embarrassed and thought that people would see me as weak. Over time, with help, and following the leadership of many others, I now know—at least in my mind, if not my heart—that I have been sick, not weak.

The good news was that my relationship with Lise was stronger than ever. Without her love and support, and the constant support of our three wonderful boys, I have no idea how I would have made it through those challenging times, and all the difficult years that preceded them. There had been so many times in the past, when I was in the depths of despair and depression, that I couldn't even imagine a future. And if there was going to be a future, I certainly didn't want to think of what it might bring. But now, the future was a tantalizing prospect—and it looked bright!

Chapter 16
Today

Every year, typically in the autumn, Lise, who is vice-president of our company, and I start discussing what we want to do both personally and professionally in the following year. This is our "Are we in the right jungle?" discussion, and it's become an important annual process for us.

In the fall of 2019, we began thinking it might be time for me to move on from full-time consulting to something else. Lise had made the transition a few years previously and was now only accepting returning sports psychology consulting clients, no new ones. She found this phase of her life, with more time to putter around the cottage and to instruct downhill skiing at Mount Tremblant, to be extremely rewarding and enjoyable.

I discussed the possibility with my private-sector manager, as was our practice, at the International Association of Chiefs of Police conference, that year being held in Chicago. After much discussion, we agreed that I would reduce my "level of effort" per month as part of a one-to-three-year strategy towards moving on.

"Forever" consultants, or consultants engaged by the same client for extended periods, should be employees, in my opinion, and I had always told their team that my goal as a consultant was to get them to the place where they no longer needed my services. I could see that we were very nearly there but still had a bit more to accomplish together before reaching that theoretical milestone. While I had mixed emotions about leaving this successful team behind after over five years, I was confident that 2020 was going to be a great year, full of other amazing opportunities and adventures.

If only we had known what 2020 would look like.

In February of that year, our team attended an outstanding CACP Technology Conference and held a hugely successful follow-on event at the beautiful Fairmont Hotel Vancouver. It was during this time that the world started to hear about something called COVID-19. We left Vancouver and took a number of the company's Canadian clients to their office in Seattle (later finding out that the city was a COVID hotbed), and I then returned home after ten days on the road.

Then COVID hit Canada—hard. Everything shut down. In team meetings, the company's three consultants (all retired law enforcement officers) advised ceasing outward communications with police leaders. They were going to be extremely busy for an extended period as they ramped up their emergency plans. A few months later, we checked with our various contacts. Would it be OK if we started to open up discussion again? The consistent answer was, "Absolutely!" While everything was shut down, these leaders had turned their vision towards key strategic initiatives they wanted to accomplish, which included moving forward with various technology and information management programs.

Just as we were becoming busy again after the first COVID lockdown, the events of May 25, 2020, in Minneapolis, Minnesota, had a cascading effect on policing—and, by extension, companies that support policing—around the world. The death of George Floyd led to

ever-increasing calls for improved police transparency and account-
ability across the United States, Canada and globally.

It is safe to say that 2020 was immensely busy and extremely demanding and provided Lise and me with cause for much soul-searching
on several fronts. Part of that soul-searching was our annual discussion about what to do personally and professionally in 2021. We had
many walks, chats and discovery exercises to help us make our decision (thank goodness for Lise and her unique skill sets). It became
clear to both of us that it was time to move on to the next victory lap.

Shortly after our decision was made, but not yet communicated
to our client, Lise did a very short but powerful exercise with me. She
asked me to close my eyes and take a few deep breaths. Then she
asked me to think for a few moments and to give her one word that
best described how I felt about the decision not to renew my contract.

I paused and said, "Resolved."

I opened my eyes and Lise was smiling. "Now, that's a powerful
word!" she said.

Telling the company team was difficult, but they were all extremely supportive of me and Lise taking this next step. I will always
be grateful to their entire team in Canada, the United States and
around the world for everything they did for me, for us. It truly was a
symbiotic relationship, which, in many cases, turned into friendships
that I will cherish for the rest of my life.

• • •

Because I was no longer returning to work as a consultant for that
particular company and was about to commence my fourth "victory
lap," I needed to put my mind to what I would be filling my time
with. I had lots of things I wanted to do in the next phase of my life,
including spending more time with our family and, once the COVID

restrictions ended, more travel and golf in the summer or winters down south or in New Zealand during their summer, our winter. I wanted to continue taking short-term contracts, especially in the area of public safety interoperability and information management. There were also a number of articles I looked forward to writing, as I enjoyed exploring my creative side. This activity would also help me to stay current and, I suppose, relevant, as best as possible.

Another creative area that I wanted to explore was playing the C flute again. I loved playing the flute when I was in high school (the only decent mark I got in five years), and I felt it would go nicely with Lise's learning the violin, something she had taken up a couple years before and was doing very well at! While this particular goal will take years to master, or at least to become decent at, I have always found playing the flute to be very relaxing and a form of meditation, both of which are excellent for a recovering alcoholic (we are always "recovering" and never truly "recovered").

I also wanted to grow my coaching practice. I've done this informally for years. While this would never be a major source of retirement funding, I thought that I had something to offer in this area. Ideally, I envisioned Lise and I doing this together, as she has a wealth of academic, sports psychology and spiritual skills and experiences to share.

Our youngest son, Mat, is in the Canadian Armed Forces and has always been in great shape. When visiting at Christmas 2020, he saw, I'm sure, that I was way overweight and totally out of shape. He gently challenged me to start working out every day and gave me a very basic plan to follow. I was happy to accept his challenge. I knew, especially after the crazy year we lived in 2020, that I was a "walking heart attack." I started the challenge on Christmas Day before our big turkey meal and, no surprise, it didn't go well. I could barely do five push-ups, and keeping a "plank" going for more than twenty seconds was impossible.

Being a believer in writing down and sharing my goals, I sat down the first week of January 2021 and wrote three major personal goals for myself. I had been mulling these over for some time and had discussed them with Lise before putting pen to paper (or fingers to keyboard):

1. Seek serenity every day.
2. Finish writing this book which is, in large part, about my daily search for serenity.
3. Within the next two years, complete an Ironman Triathlon. (Originally, I gave myself one year to achieve this, but Lise gently reminded me that goals need to be attainable—and I would certainly need at least two years to attain this one!)

Most importantly, I wanted to move from being the kind of person who is always thinking "What's next?" to the type of person, like my beautiful wife, who lives life to the fullest, one day at a time. It was time not only to continue planning for our future but also to stop and smell the roses.

•   •   •

Although I drafted the outline for this book a few years ago, I didn't begin the process of writing it until the first week of January 2021. With very few exceptions, I woke up at 7 a.m. or earlier every weekday and, after making a cup of tea, sat in my office chair to look out over the lake, both for the peace it brings and for inspiration. I would then say the Serenity Prayer and, as much as my spinning mind would allow, take a few moments in the hope that I could achieve goal number one, finding serenity.

I typically started writing by around 7:15 and would have an alarm set for 8:20 to remind me to stop writing for the day. Sometimes, if I was in the middle of a story, I would continue for another ten or fifteen minutes, never longer. While this measured approach slowed down the process of drafting this book, it also allowed me the time to take the creative process, such as it was, slowly and methodically.

I also wanted to be sure that writing didn't become a new addiction and take over my life. With that in mind, Lise and I often sat together around 8:30 for a chat, prayer and meditation. This, too, is an important part of our joint "retirement," and helps to keep me centred and aware of the most important relationship in my life.

On writing days, I wouldn't look at my phone, email, text messages or social media (or any of the other distractions that drove my life for so many years) until that morning routine was complete. It was wonderful being free of those "Pavlovian dog" types of mental triggers in my life, especially first thing in the morning.

Somewhere along the line, I amended my Ironman goal, realizing that the amount of training it required would mean too much time away from Lise and the rest of the family. I committed to a half-Ironman instead but would still need to work on my physical strength and discipline. I started jogging at the end of January 2021 and, by May, was running four kilometres three times a week. Not fast, as I never was fast, but without stopping, and I felt winded but good after each run.

I continued to ramp up my training, working out about fifteen hours a week and following a number of cardio, strength, core and yoga programs to be ready for my half-Ironman in 2022. Lise and I also went cross-country skiing a number of times in the winter of 2021, and we walked together most days. She gently reminded me that even with my healthy focus on my physical fitness and endurance, it was important for me to keep everything in balance, something I have always struggled with.

Our lives had truly become much more interdependent. Although Lise had numerous activities and friends that kept her busy and I was focused on writing and getting back in shape physically, we made sure to find "couple time" most days and even put key dates in our calendars to ensure we checked in with each other to compare notes on how we were doing with regard to nurturing our relationship.

•   •   •

Do you remember this paragraph from Chapter 5?

> *This, dear reader, is the crux of this story. Not my policing career with a few, I hope, funny stories along the way. Not even my love story with Lise. No, this story (some might call it a tragedy) is about how a nice young man, from a good family, with a pretty normal upbringing, changes into someone so dark, so ugly, so mean-spirited, so disrespectful and, ultimately, so broken. So broken that he almost loses everything—including his life at his own hands.*

What I didn't tell you then was that this is also a story of redemption. Of healing. Of forgiveness. And, ultimately, of making it out of the valley of darkness and climbing to the peaks of the mountains of peace and, from time to time, true serenity.

Today, I realize that I was not down, I was depressed. I've never formally been diagnosed with depression, but there's no doubt that it has afflicted me. I still feel this way from time to time, but thankfully, I am now able to sense it coming on and take positive steps to lessen its impact. These steps include letting Lise know right away so that she can be supportive. Where necessary, I also ensure that I am looking after my "HALT" symptoms by eating healthily (when I'm hungry), managing my emotions (when I'm angry), pushing myself to engage with Lise and/or family (when I'm lonely) and getting lots of sleep, sometimes taking two naps in a day (when I'm tired).

While Lise is massively supportive, as are our boys and their partners, there are still times when she will say something like, "Why can't you snap out of it?" She means well, as do others who think this way; but, as I explain to her, it's not like there is a switch I can control for my depression or anxiety. It sneaks up on me, and before I know it, I'm already feeling down, teetering on the precipice of depression. The good news is that my early warning systems allow me to identify the symptoms, to help myself avoid sinking any further, and to ask Lise or the boys for their help as well.

Fortunately, the anxious feelings that began in 2017, after my first detached retina, have pretty much abated. Although I still have feelings of anxiety that begin to well up in my chest from time to time, they have been very mild, and I'm able to use the breathing techniques my counsellor taught me with great success. Lately, the only health-related issues I've had to deal with have been a touch of gout, a fairly mild diverticulitis incident that I was able to manage with rest and diet and, of course, the constant ringing in my ear. While some of those issues set me back a bit with regard to my training, they were manageable with the fitness equipment we have at the cottage.

•   •   •

In Chapter 12, "Begin with the End in Mind," I wrote about the Twelve Promises and listed them. I'm very happy to say that I have, for the most part, achieved them. The one promise I continue to struggle with is number two: "We will not regret the past nor wish to shut the door on it." I'm afraid that I have never stopped regretting the past—my past self, my past behaviours and the damage they did to my family relationships. Even now, after all the work, the forgiveness and the redemption, I still desperately wish that I could go back and change things. Clearly, this is something I need to keep seeking professional help with.

I also recognize that my anger and aggressive behaviours towards our children, even in their teenage years, have likely impacted them negatively. They may not even be fully cognizant of these traumas, or ready to deal with them yet. While I hugely regret all the pain that I've caused them, I'm one hundred percent committed to continuing to work on myself and supporting them in their adult journeys in any way I can. Finding ways to end these negative legacies is crucial in the years I have left.

On a much more positive note, Promise Five states, "No matter how far down the scale we have gone, we will see how our experience can benefit others." I believe this book is the manifestation of that promise. This book is also, in part, my way of continuing to fulfil the twelfth step in AA: "Having had a spiritual awakening as the result of these Steps, we tried to carry this message to alcoholics, and to practice these principles in all our affairs."

· · ·

I was talking with a friend one day as I neared completion of the first draft of this book. My friend was still working full-time in a very stressful career and spent about twenty minutes telling me all the things that were going wrong at work: the lack of support from a particular team, the inaction by organization leaders, the feelings of frustration with it all. As I sat there, listening to them pour out their feelings and concerns, I couldn't help but smile. Not because I was not empathetic towards their situation; of course, I felt sorry for what they were going through. No, I smiled because the most frustration I feel in my life today is that I'm not losing weight as quickly as I would like or that I don't have more time to read books on days that I have a heavy training schedule.

My life, our life, is extremely good. Even in the face of one of the world's worst pandemics when neither of us were able to work, we got by fine for three months with no extra money coming in. With our pensions as the only source of income, we made it through each month with money left in our chequing account. Today, we still have pretty much everything we want, and if we decide to head south for a month or so next year, we can certainly afford it. Gone is the gnawing financial stress that caused so many problems in our earlier years.

Lise and I are in a wonderful space with regard to our relationship. While we are both busy with our own individual interests, we are nicely interdependent and deeply in love, and we treat each other with kindness and respect. All a far cry from where we were on that fateful day in January 2006 when Lise showed such strength and courage in telling me that I needed to leave. Thank God she did that. And thank God for the previous twenty-five years of sobriety and our constant and never-ending willingness to fight for our relationship.

"There but for the grace of God" is an AA slogan and something I often say when I see someone struggling or hear about a story of addiction, suicide, depression or other mental health–related challenge. While Lise and I will always face these challenges ourselves, we now have the faith, tools, experience and support we need to make it through the valley of despair and to continue climbing to the peaks of happiness and joy in our beautiful marriage.

•   •   •

February 2, 2021, was my twenty-fifth "birthday" in Alcoholics Anonymous. Twenty-five years since I had the courage to admit my addiction and take responsibility for overcoming it. That day, after much thought and reflection, and after first discussing my idea with Lise and the boys, I decided to share my story publicly for the first time. The thought was extremely scary for me, as the vast majority of people who knew me up to that point had no idea that I'm an alcoholic. They had no clue about the mean, horrible person I had become in my private life because of my addiction and how cruelly I treated the ones I loved the most. However, I judged that it was the right time to open up, and I hoped that my sharing might help others, just as I hope this book will do.

Lise and the boys all agreed and thought it was a good idea, so I published a short article on LinkedIn titled "Speaking Out about Mental Health and Wellness: My 25th Birthday in AA." Here is a key section from it:

I'm here today because Lise got help and set boundaries. And because, thank God, I took the first step and kept working on my sobriety, one day at a time, 9,125 days in a row and still counting.

Ultimately, though, I'm here because of God's grace and love. It's OK if you don't believe in God, use a different name for your "higher power" or don't believe in any of these things.

However, twenty-five years of experience tell me that trying to get better on your own, thinking you don't need anyone else or some external help will, in all likelihood, not end well.

The response, literally from around the world, was both powerful and extremely touching. Hundreds of people, most of whom I know and many I don't, took the time to either react to the post or write heartfelt comments. The outpouring of support and the depth of warmth that was shared reassured me that I had made the right decision in sharing my story.

More importantly, though, I received a number of private messages via LinkedIn and various other platforms (I also posted a link to the story on Twitter) from people telling me their stories of addiction and mental health challenges, or stories about family members who were struggling. I hope the messages I shared directly with them have, in some small way, helped. I will likely never know what impact my story has on others, either via that post or this book. I can only hope that sharing about our journey will help others, and possibly even help save lives and families.

• • •

As I stated at the outset of this book, my goal in writing it was first and foremost an attempt to understand the "why" of my life. Why did a fairly normal young boy who grew up in a good family become the monster he did? However, writing this book was also a way to apologize to Lise and the boys, once again, for all the hurt, suffering and pain I caused them. They have all forgiven me, many times, but I continue to struggle with forgiving myself.

An obvious extension of the "why" journey is the corresponding "how" journey—how to become the loving husband, father, son, brother, friend and person I was meant to be. These two journeys combined may just lead to the promised land of hope. Hope for a positive future filled with respect, patience, love and maybe, just maybe, acceptance.

If you are not a member of my family, you are reading this book only because my family has given me permission to publish it. Their permission unlocks my fourth and final goal: to share my story in the hope that it might help you, the reader. If you are struggling, seek help. If you live with someone who is struggling, seek help. No matter how bad things are, they can get better, but not if you try to do it on your own.

There are, thankfully, tons of resources out there today to help. If alcohol is the problem, there are, of course, Alcoholics Anonymous (www.aa.org) and Al-Anon (al-anon.org). In the Giving Back section at the end of this book, you'll find other wonderful resources that provide incredible life-saving support, some of it specifically to police officers. No matter what your walk of life may be, the key is taking the first step to help, health and recovery.

Please take it.

Today.

Chapter 17

Tomorrow

I have come such a long way on my journey with addiction and mental health. I used to wonder how I would ever get through each day and if there would even be a tomorrow. And Lise and I struggled for so long going from hurt to hurt before we could find the patience, respect and forgiveness to move beyond all that to a stronger, more loving future together. We have learned to embrace and enjoy the present moment, and we still have so much to look forward to. I can't wait for family trips, stopping for coffee or a picnic lunch along the highway, playing golf with the kids and, hopefully soon, totally spoiling our grandchildren with love (and sweets when their parents aren't looking).

Mental and physical health permitting, Lise and I have tons of amazing trips to plan and experience, including swapping houses with a friend in New Zealand; taking a family trip to Hawaii and watching our children and their partners experience the majesty, power and serenity of a Haleakalā sunrise (and the great fun coasting on bikes down the mountain afterward); taking our first river cruise in Europe (we've cruised big ships in the Atlantic, Pacific, Caribbean and Mediterranean but have never done a small river cruise); and finally taking the year-long North American RV trip we have long dreamed of, starting in Ottawa one April and slowly going west, then north, then south before the snow flies and then east along the bottom of United States, only to head north again the following spring.

In the meantime, we are fortunate enough to live in a wonderful lakefront home. Staying here, enjoying all that God and nature have to offer and welcoming visitors, ideally from around the world, is always at the top of our "to do" list. Lise will continue working on her personal goals and I will continue working on mine, hopefully with that ever-elusive serenity being achieved on a regular basis.

•　•　•

I want to close with wise words from the character William Parrish, played by Anthony Hopkins, in one of my favourite movies, *Meet Joe Black*:

> *I want you to get swept away. I want you to levitate. I want you to sing with rapture and dance like a dervish. Be deliriously happy. I know it's a cornball thing, but love is passion, obsession, someone you can't live without. If you don't start with that, what are you going to end up with? I say fall head over heels. Find someone you can love like crazy and who'll love you the same way back. And how do you find him? Forget your head and listen to your heart. Run the risk. If you get hurt, you'll come back. Because the truth is, there is no sense living your life without this. To make the journey and not fall deeply in love—well, you haven't lived a life at all. You have to try. Because if you haven't tried, you haven't lived.[16]*

---

16. Courtesy of Universal Studios Licensing LLC

I've been extremely blessed to find that kind of love in my life with Lise. Hopefully we have our health for many more years to enjoy it for as long as we possibly can.

Here's to living life to its fullest and being deliriously happy every day!

Lance Valcour

Ma belle petite crotte de nez
(Lise's Journey)

by Lance Valcour

Beautiful soul
Beautiful spirit
Soaring energy
Soaring freedom
Joining love
Joining forever
Broken energy
Broken freedom
Caged soul
Caged spirit
Resolute will
Resolute vision
Forever fighting
Forever seeking
Cresting mountains
Cresting peaks
Breaking sunrise
Breaking joy
Beautiful soul
Beautiful spirit

Note: I had never written a poem before, but this one came to me all at once, unbidden, and I wrote it down in five minutes on September 27, 2024, after finishing the second round of substantive edits on the book manuscript.

Giving Back

I have been fortunate to receive life-saving help and support from a number of individuals and organizations in my journey of recovery. Now, it's my turn to pay some of that forward to three very special charities.

Serenity Renewal for Families
www.serenityrenewal.ca

Twenty percent of the net profits from this book will go to support Serenity Renewal for Families, a small non-profit whose mission is:

> *To provide hope and support in a safe environment through short-term counselling, educational workshops and programs for individuals and families affected directly or indirectly by addictions.*

For over forty years Serenity Renewal for Families has been helping support families in the Ottawa area who are in recovery, and they are just a phone call away (613-523-5143). They helped save my life and they may be able to support your family too.

Canada Beyond The Blue

www.canadabeyondtheblue.com

Twenty percent of the net profits from this book will go to support Canada Beyond The Blue, whose mission and vision are:

Committed to providing a community of support to police members and their families, through resources that will provide education, peer support and practical tools to enable families to thrive in their roles as the support system for their police member.

Badge of Life Canada

www.badgeoflifecanada.org

Twenty percent of the net profits from this book will go to support Badge of Life Canada, which was originally started by an Ottawa Police officer and whose mission is:

Empowering Canadian Public Safety personnel and their families who are dealing with operational stress injuries, including post-traumatic stress and suicidal ideation, to achieve healthy living and post-traumatic growth.

About the Author

Inspector (Ret.) Lance Valcour O.O.M. retired from the Ottawa Police Service in 2010 after thirty-three years of service. He is an author, an independent consultant, a strategic advisor, a marketing technologist, a digital evangelist, a coach, an internationally recognized keynote speaker and a facilitator on a wide range of public safety issues, including information management, information and communications technology, interoperability and business development.

Lance was invested as an Officer of the Order of Merit of the Police Forces by the Governor General of Canada in 2010 and received the Queen's Diamond Jubilee Medal in 2012. In May 2019, Lance received the 2019 Ontario Women in Law Enforcement's Presidential Award, one of few men to receive this prestigious award.

Lance has been married to Lise, whose inner strength and courage inspired *If They Only Knew*, for thirty-nine years. They have three sons and three grandsons. Lance is currently writing his next book, tentatively titled *What's Next: A Guide to Value-Based Decisions*.

Website: lancevalcour.com
X (Twitter): x.com/Lance_Valcour
Facebook: www.facebook.com/profile.php?id=61559569108783
LinkedIn: www.linkedin.com/in/
inspector-ret-lance-valcour-o-o-m-b3585314/

If you've found this book helpful in your journey, please consider posting a review on Amazon, Goodreads or other online book platforms. It would be wonderful to hear how the book might have helped and, frankly, a positive review will help push sales, ensuring that Canada Beyond The Blue, Badge of Life Canada and Serenity Renewal for Families continue to receive proceeds from book sales. Your support is greatly appreciated!

www.ingramcontent.com/pod-product-compliance
Lightning Source LLC
Chambersburg PA
CBHW030411130626
46549CB00004B/1721